Coming to Law School

Coming to Law School

How to Prepare Yourself for the Next Three Years

Ian Gallacher

CAROLINA ACADEMIC PRESS

Durham, North Carolina

Library of Congress Cataloging-in-Publication Data

Gallacher, Ian, 1956-
  Coming to law school : how to prepare yourself for the next three years / Ian
Gallacher.
    p. cm.
  ISBN 978-1-59460-653-3 (alk. paper)
  1. Law students--United States--Handbooks, manuals, etc. 2. Law--Study
and teaching--United States. 3. Law--Vocational guidance--United States. I.
Title.

  KF283.G35 2010
  340.071'173--dc22

                                    2009048883

CAROLINA ACADEMIC PRESS
700 Kent Street
Durham, North Carolina 27701
Telephone (919) 489-7486
Fax (919) 493-5668
www.cap-press.com

Printed in the United States of America

*To Julie McKinstry, who helped when I came
to law school and who has helped every day before and since*

Contents

Acknowledgments

No project like this comes about without the work of many people, and I need to thank them for their help and support. In particular, I thank the students who wrote to me with suggestions about what they would like to see in a document like this. I also thank my colleagues in the LCR program at Syracuse—Professors Elizabeth August, Elton Fukumoto, Andrew Greenberg, Susan James, Lynn Levey, Aliza Milner, Kathleen O'Connor, Lucille Rignanese, and Richard Risman, who have helped me think about many of these issues, and Lynn Oatman for her administrative help. Professor Risman also read an early draft and offered helpful suggestions, for which I'm particularly grateful. Thanks to Dean Hannah Arterian and Associate Dean Tomas Gonzalez for their interest and support. And thanks to my students, who always help me see things in ways I hadn't considered. Thanks in particular to Jennifer Pautz for her research help. And thanks to my parents, Joan Upton-Holder and Henry Gallacher, and my step-father, Roy Upton-Holder, who all made it possible for me to come to law school. As always, this book is for Julie McKinstry.

Coming to Law School

1

Introduction

Welcome to law school and to the practice of law. The administration, faculty, and staff of your law school are all delighted you're coming to spend the next three years with them. The start of a law school year is a particularly exciting time for everyone, largely because of first-year students like you; you have a great deal of energy and excitement about finally getting down to the study of law, and that excitement affects everyone around you.

That said, the start of an academic year means a lot of administrative work to be done, and it's easy for everyone in law school—incoming students, upperclass students, staff, administration, and faculty—to be so wrapped up in the details of getting the year going that some things are left unsaid. So let me say a few of them here. You should be very proud of your accomplishments in getting this far in your academic career. Despite all the talk about how many lawyers we have in this country, a law degree is still a difficult qualification to obtain, and you've taken the biggest step toward getting one by being admitted to law school. Sure, you have to earn passing grades in all your courses over the next three years, but the vast majority of you will do that and will graduate with a law degree three (or four perhaps, if you take a dual degree) years from now. And yes, there's the bar exam to take before you can actually practice law, but the vast majority of you will pass that soon after you graduate, and then you'll be lawyers.

Even though you're not formally lawyers yet, I welcomed you to the practice of law, and I meant it. It's not too early to start thinking of yourselves as lawyers, even though you won't actually get to be fully fledged practitioners for a few years. Some of you will work in a clinic or as interns or externs while in law school, and the work you do will be on behalf of clients who have a pressing need for excellent legal work. Certainly you'll be earning academic credit for the work you do, and you'll be supervised more closely, perhaps, than practicing lawyers, but the work you do—and the effect that work has on people—will be no different than if you were licensed to practice. Similarly, some of you will work in your first- or second-year summer in a paid position for a law firm or other entity. There you'll be, for all practical purposes, doing the same work as that done by practicing lawyers. Even if you don't do any of these things, you'll probably represent hypothetical clients in your legal research and writing classes from early in the first semester. You'll be expected to show the same client-centered and professional behavior on behalf of those hypothetical people as you would be expected to show actual clients.

A high degree of professionalism is going to be expected of you from your first days in law school through to graduation and, of course, into your lives as lawyers. That expectation extends to the way you approach everything you do in law school. Put simply, law school isn't like anything else you've experienced in your academic careers. Your professors will all have high expectations of you and will expect you to handle a lot of work. You can and probably will get through law school and even thrive, but you'll have to take your work seriously.

In fact, the best way to think of law school is not as school at all, but as a job. If you take your classes as seriously as you undoubtedly would take a job at a major law firm and approach the work for those classes with the same measure of determination and energy as you would an assignment from a partner at that firm, you will almost certainly do very well. But if you treat your classes with the disengaged apathy that some undergraduate students display — especially after an evening of social activities — then law school will be, at best, a struggle for you. It's up to you, but I'm guessing that given the choice, most of you would prefer to do well in law school, and not many of you would volunteer to go through this sometimes difficult and always expensive experience to do poorly. The good news is that you're certainly smart enough to thrive in law school, so the power to do well here is pretty much entirely within your own control.

Well. It's impolite to speak to someone without introducing yourself so please let me do that now. I am Ian Gallacher. I'm an Associate Professor at the Syracuse University College of Law, and I'm the director of the legal research and writing program there. I came to teaching from a law practice in Baltimore, where I was a partner in a litigation firm. My practice was mainly concerned with complex civil litigation, defending clients against class action suits and multidistrict litigation. Before practice and after graduating from law school, I clerked for a federal district judge in Baltimore for two years. Before going to law school, I was a classical musician; I conducted orchestras and played violin and viola. There's more to me than that brief sketch, of course, but that's enough about me for now.

I tell you these things about myself because I want to make clear that I know what you're feeling as you prepare for law school. I know what it's like to get through law school and practice law. When I went to law school, I only had the vaguest idea about how the law worked, and that knowledge — if it can be called that—was acquired mainly from TV shows about lawyers. I had no idea about what law school was like, other than the terrifying impression left by some books that described the miserable life of first-year law students.

It was not even close to being as bad as I feared or as bad as maybe you think it will be. Law school can certainly be a mysterious place sometimes, and the things you'll be studying, and the way you'll be studying them, might seem foreign to you for a while. Don't worry; almost everyone is confused when they come to law school—even the students who look as if they know exactly what they're doing—and hardly anyone is confused by the time exams come around. The Socratic teaching method is much more benign than you might have been led to believe.

I've often been asked what an incoming student can do to prepare for law school, and my standard answer has always been the same as what I was told: there really isn't a good way to get ready for the experience. Just come to law school rested and ready to study, and everything will take care of itself. I'm no longer sure that's the best answer, because there are some things you could do before you come to school to get ready for the experience of being a law student, and you'll probably have an easier transition from your previous life to your life as a law student if you do those things.

One thing is certainly true: you shouldn't start studying the law over the summer. That's what law school is for, and it's much better for you to wait until you meet your teachers and learn what they want you to learn. As you'll discover, the law is such a big subject—even within the discrete areas like torts, contracts, criminal law, and so on—that different teachers will emphasize different things. Some teachers prefer to look at the law from one perspective, whereas others will look at things a different way. You want to learn the way your professors want you to because they'll be setting and grading the exams you take at the end of the semester.

There are some skills, though, you could work on over the summer; simple things that will nonetheless help you tremendously when the pressure of law school starts to build up. If you've refined some of these basic skills, you'll be able to handle that pressure much more effectively.

I've written this introduction to law school and some of the skills you'll need to thrive here in order to help you make the transition from your present life to your life as a law student. Some of the information here might seem very basic, even childish. I can only tell you that I'm putting into this book those things I think law school students could use and that some, at least, don't know when they come to school. Even if you're confident of your study skills, there's probably something in here you don't know or have forgotten. Now's the time to remember or learn these things; there's no pressure on you to perform, you're not struggling to keep up with the reading for the week, and you don't have a complicated writing assignment due any time soon.

There won't be any discussion here about substantive legal issues; there's time enough for that when you meet your torts, contracts, and other teachers in law school. Although we'll spend a little time considering some basic civics information that will be helpful to give you some initial context for the things you'll be learning later on, my primary emphasis is on the skills you need to assimilate, record, and report information—listening, reading, and writing—and time management skills to keep yourself on track. These are skills you've already refined to an extent in your school and previous university careers, but you'll almost certainly have to improve them now that you're in law school.

All of this is voluntary for you. No one is going to test you on any of this material, and your course work at law school is not going to be dependent on your having learned anything over the summer. Although I've included some exercises in case you want to try your hand at practicing some skills, no one is going to grade those exercises or even want to see that you've done them. On the other hand, the more you read and think about the things I'm going to talk about, the more relaxed you'll be on the first day of law school, and anything that reduces your stress level on that day is a good thing. I suspect that those of you who read all of this and work on some of the exercises will do better in law school than those who don't. That's because in general, the more refined your skills are, and the more confident you are in those skills, the better you'll do in law school and in the practice of law.

The principal reason I hope you'll read and work through the material in this book, though, is that it will help you to learn the law. Behind the pomp and circumstance of law school ceremonies, and behind the mysteries of the Socratic method and the other teaching techniques your professors will use, is a simple truth that isn't often expressed: your professors will not teach you the law. Rather, they'll show you how to teach yourself the law, and they'll guide you down the path that leads to knowledge of the law. The burden, however, is on you to learn, and the skills talked about here will help you do that.

It's not just in law school that these skills are important. It's possible that you'll have spent little or no time in law school studying the particular legal doctrine that will become important to you in practice. That's understandable, of course; the law's a vast field, and neither you nor your teachers can be sure what part of it you'll be working in after graduation. So we try to get you ready for practice by teaching you how the law works generally, and we trust to your study and learning skills to help you learn the specifics of your practice area once you're in practice. That's why these study skills and the communication skills of reading, writing, research, and oral presentation you'll learn in your legal research and writing classes are so important; they are the skills that will help you find out about and communicate your knowledge of your chosen area of the law.

It's important to note that everything I say here is my opinion and my opinion only. Some of your professors might agree with some of what I say here, some might disagree with some of it, and some—not many, I hope—will disagree with a lot. That's fine; everyone's entitled to opinions, and if we all agreed on everything, life would not only be boring, there wouldn't be many jobs for lawyers. But if, once you get to school, you get the sense that your professor wants you to do something other than the way it's described here—brief a case, for example, or take notes—then you should do exactly what your professor wants. This is a general guide; what your professor tells you is specific. Specific always wins out over general.

My guiding principle in writing this has been to tell you some of the things I wish I had known before I came to law school. My life as a law student would have been a lot simpler, and a lot less stressed, if I'd known some of these things, or even if someone had told them to me once I was in law school. I had to figure most of this out on my own, and some things I didn't know until years after I left school. I would have been a better law student—and maybe a better lawyer—if I'd been told these things before I came to school. I hope you feel the same way and that at least some of this information helps you in law school, or at least helps you be more relaxed as you approach three of the most challenging and enjoyable years of your life.

For those of you who are going to continue, let's talk a little about what you'll be doing and why you'll be doing it.

2

Quick Overview

I said earlier that we'd be talking here about some fundamental skills—reading, listening, writing, and managing your time—and that's the bulk of what we'll be doing. It may not sound very challenging, but I need to be blunt—you're not as good at these skills as you think you are. I'm confident in making this claim because it's true of *all* incoming law students. You've excelled academically all your lives, and for most of you, that excellence has come easily. So it's easy for you to assume that you already know how to do something and that you don't need to work on improving a skill you first learned when you were much younger. It's better to start weaning yourself from these mistaken beliefs sooner rather than later, certainly before law school proves to you the hard way that your assumptions were wrong.

We'll look first at reading, and in particular we'll talk about how lawyers read and derive information from texts. You might be skeptical about this and may think to yourself that you obviously know how to read and that you've done pretty well academically with your current reading skills. And you're right, of course. You might also be skeptical about the notion that lawyers read any differently from those who study in other academic disciplines, and you might be right about that as well.

What's different is that we expect you to read at the highest level of concentration and attention to detail, and we expect you to never deviate from that standard. I doubt you've been held to that degree of total concentration for long periods of time, and you need to get used to the fact that in your professional career at least, you'll never be allowed to read anything with less than a total commitment to suck all possible relevant information out of a piece of writing.

Next, we'll talk about briefing, the practice of taking notes about what you're reading in such a way that the notes will be useful to you in the short and long term. Law students take notes about their reading for two main reasons: they don't want to be humiliated in class when their teacher asks them about the reading and they have to answer in front of a room full of their colleagues, and they want to do well on exams, which ask them to recall details of cases they read months ago. Good notes can help with both of those goals, and they can help focus your reading as well. We'll discuss the symbiotic relationship between reading and briefing, and we'll talk about why that relationship is often misunderstood by law students.

Then we'll discuss listening in class and how to take notes about what you hear. Again, this might seem elementary to someone who has performed at a very high academic level, at school as undergraduates, and perhaps as graduate students as well, but law school is a very different place. No matter how well you've done elsewhere, there's always room to do better; I can assure you that law school will demand an improvement from all of you. The good news is that improvement is not only possible, it's virtually guaranteed if you put in a little work.

We'll also talk about outlining, the technique by which you take all your briefs and class notes and turn them into a comprehensive review of a particular subject. It's an important step that helps you cement what you've learned firmly into your memory, and it's much mythologized by books, movies, and TV shows having to do with life in law school. If you've taken good, careful notes before and during class, outlining is a fairly straightforward and uncomplicated process.

Then we'll talk about writing. We won't spend much time talking about specific techniques you can use to make your writing better—that's what your legal writing classes are for. We will talk about the fact that many believe that law students and junior lawyers don't write very well, and we'll try to get some perspective on that perception. We'll talk in general about what good writing might be and why it's important. There isn't much time to talk about these topics in class, and it will be helpful for you to think a little more broadly about the importance of writing to you as a law student and as a lawyer.

To wrap up this discussion of practical skills, we'll talk a little about time management. If you do everything I recommend, you're going to feel that you have no time for anything in your life but your law school work, and perhaps you'll believe that there isn't even enough time for that. But it's not true. Your school work will certainly take up a lot of time, but you have to work for some balance in your life. Good time management skills can help you carve out some time in your schedule for the people and the non-law school activities that are important to you.

Because many students come to law school with only a vague understanding of some of the important civics information that will help them understand what their teachers are talking about when they speak of the role of Congress or the President in the legal process or about the influence one court's decision might have on other courts, I've included a brief discussion of these issues. This isn't intended as a substitute for the more intensive study of these questions you'll engage in while in law school, and many of you may know much more about all of this than I've mentioned here. For those of you without much of a grounding in these issues, though, the discussion here should be enough to keep you in the conversation once you get to law school.

Where appropriate, I've included exercises for you to work on. As I said previously, no one is going to check up on you to see if you've done these exercises or not. They're included to give you the chance to practice the skills we're talking about and, as with so many things at law school, it's up to you to decide whether you need that practice. What's important is that you be honest and realistic with yourself and approach this with an open mind.

3

Reading

Many think that the act of reading is simple: the eye moves from the top left corner of the page to the bottom right corner, and then on to the next page, and then on and on to the end of the document. The eye always moves forward, not backward, and when it reaches the end, it stops. Of course, there's an element of truth to that. In English, we do read from left to right and top to bottom, so to read a document from start to finish, you do have to read all the words in that order.

But if that's the only way we read, we're reading passively, and passive reading is not a good way to learn something. Perhaps it's fine if we're reading something purely for entertainment, while lying in a deck chair on the beach, say, or cruising at altitude in an airplane. If we're reading something to learn, though, it's crucial that we become active readers, and that means a very different reading style.

Active reading is not at all like the left to right, top to bottom, front to back style. When you read actively, you stop, think about what you've just read, think about what you read previously, go back to reread what you read some pages ago to compare it with what you just read, and jump back to where you stopped reading. You repeat this process often. You constantly ask yourself whether you agree with what you've read and whether it makes sense based on what you've learned previously about this subject and based on your own life experience. You ask questions of the text as well. What is the writer trying to tell you here? What will come next? Where have you heard this before? What, in short, is being communicated by this text?

Active reading is like a conversation between you and the writer. The writer has something to say and has actively organized the material carefully and thoughtfully, but the writer doesn't know you and therefore can't calibrate the document specifically to the way you learn. The writer has done the work a writer can do, but the rest of the work is up to you. You have to engage in the document, think about what's being said, and do everything you can to learn as much as possible from the text. A good writer is hoping you'll engage the text and will therefore choose words carefully, in the hope that you will appreciate the nuances of the writing and interpret the deeper messages embedded in the fabric of the text, as well as the superficial information. A good writer, in short, wants to talk to you and have you talk back, engaging in a two-way conversation through the medium of the text.

There's a tremendous amount of that deeper information embedded into legal texts. They're packed full of information, coiled into the documents like a jack-in-the-box, ready to spring up as soon as you turn the page. The amount of information contained in even a short court decision can be remarkable, and you're going to be responsible for understanding as much of it as possible.

It's not just the text that gives you information. There's a lot of data to be gleaned from context and subtext as well, and it's your job to learn all of that as well. There's a tremendous amount of information you can derive from the tone a legal writer uses, the length of sentences in a particular piece of writing, and the words used to express a point.

We'll take a look at all of this in more detail later. For now, though, here's an exercise that should help you practice your active reading skills.

> **Exercise:** Buy a paper edition of a newspaper each day, and read at least two sections, one of which should be the editorial section. Read each story and editorial actively; stop after each sentence and think about how it added to your knowledge of the story's subject; ask yourself if you agree with the point the writer is making; ask if the writer has supported a point with sufficient authority or is trying to disguise the fact that there isn't any support for the position being advocated. How does the writer really feel about this subject or the people described in the story? Can you predict what the writer will say in the next sentence? Were you right? Try to draw out every element of information from the writing, every nuance of meaning, every detail. If you really devote yourself to this exercise, you might feel tired when you're finished, as if you'd done physical instead of mental exercise. Just like with physical exercise, if you do this regularly, you'll find it getting easier.

A. Active Reading and Law Students

You might be wondering why all this matters to you. Sure, you can see that being able to unpack all the information crammed in a legal text would be helpful, but if you just get the basics—the rule, say, and maybe the facts that led the court to articulate the rule—wouldn't that be enough to get by? The rest of that information might be nice to know, but does it really matter that much to you?

Yes, it does. There's been some excellent research done on reading in law school, and it demonstrates without room for doubt that how a student reads has a direct effect on that student's grades. I haven't met any law students who came to law school with the intention of doing poorly, so I probably have your undivided attention at the moment.

I'm not going to worry you with a description of how less successful students read. Instead, here's a summary of successful reading strategies. If you read using these strategies and concentrate on how and what you're reading, I can virtually promise you that you'll do better in law school than someone who just reads from left to right, top to bottom.

1. Read for a Reason

Many students read a text with no clear reason for doing so, other than it is required reading for a course. Don't read anything without a clear purpose in mind. Ask yourself what information you would want to derive from this text if you were a judge who was asked to rule on a set of facts very similar to the ones presented by a case; or imagine you are a lawyer representing either the plaintiff or the defendant in that case. Even better, ask yourself how you would read the case if you were a law school professor; why would you tell your students to read this text, how does it fit with what your students already know about a topic, and how would it advance the conversation? It might seem like an artificial process to put yourself into someone's shoes as you're reading a text, but reading for a reason—other than to check off an assignment on a to-do list—is a highly effective way to engage your brain and to get yourself reading actively.

2. Place the Case in Context

Cases don't exist in a vacuum, isolated from history, doctrine, or the continuum of litigation concerning a particular set of facts. Don't just read the words of the case itself, think about the context from which the case arose.

For example, you should ask yourself if this is a state or federal case, and what difference (if any) the answer might make to the significance and precedential value of the case. Ask if the case is from a trial court, intermediate appellate court, or court of last resort, and again reflect on what, if any, difference the answer makes to the importance of the case. On whom is the court's decision binding, and on whom is it just persuasive authority? From what jurisdiction does the case come? Societal values in, say, California and Alabama might differ on some issues, so consider whether the case fits within or stands apart from your perceptions of the social and moral values of various jurisdictions around the country. Consider when the case was decided. A case from 100 years ago might not have been directly overruled and might therefore continue to be good law, but the assumptions underlying the court's decision might no longer be valid, weakening the case's importance. What might those assumptions be? Does the opinion tell you?

All of this contextual information is crucial to an understanding of what the court is saying and why. Thinking about these issues will help you reach a deeper understanding of the text.

3. *Answer Any Questions You Have before Moving On*

You should be asking the text questions all the time, and you should answer those questions to your satisfaction before moving on to the next passage of text. This is a crucial reading strategy, and it lies at the heart of active reading. Many of these questions are simple and can be answered very quickly; some might be more complicated and take more time to consider and answer. But it's time well spent, because the more you think about every detail in whatever you're reading, the more engaged you are with the text and the more likely you are to understand and be able to remember the text. Answering your questions might require you to use an external source, like a general or legal dictionary, to explain words or phrases you don't understand, or you might refer to internal passages in the text—passages you've already read or (less frequently), passages that are yet to come. The important thing is to answer every question that comes up before moving on and be rigorous in both your questioning and your evaluation of your answers. If your answer won't hold up to the scrutiny of your professor in class, it isn't good enough for your purposes now either, so you need to rethink your answer before you move on.

4. *Don't Read on Automatic Pilot*

This strategy should be obvious if you've been paying attention, because you can't employ the other reading techniques without full engagement with the text. It's still worth saying that you can't let your attention wander, even for a word or two. Most cases contain the same or similar elements, and many of them might appear to have been written without much thought. But there is information in everything, and even if the writer wasn't considerate enough to make that information easy to access, it's your job to mine the information from the text. You should read every word, sentence, paragraph, and section critically and carefully.

There are other things you can do to improve your textual interpretive skills—make sure you have time to read everything thoroughly and more than once, read in a well-lit and comfortable environment, and keep external sources of distraction, like music or text messages that interrupt you, to a minimum. If you follow the four reading strategies outlined here, you're almost guaranteed to do better in law school than you would if you picked up a book, read quickly through the assigned reading, and assumed that you had "done the reading" for the next class.

B. Active Reading in Action

As you can imagine, active reading uncovers many layers of meaning in writing. Let's start at the top and work our way down. We'll be looking at court decisions as we investigate how to read like a lawyer. That's not because cases are more important than statutes or regulations—in fact, the opposite is becoming more true as legislatures move to codify matters that used to be left to courts and the common law. But court opinions are generally more textured and nuanced in their language than statutes are, and they are also the type of writing you'll encounter most often as first-year law students, so they are ideal for our purposes here.

It's worth making an important caveat at this point. Even though cases are the type of writing you encounter most often in your first year of law school, you should *not* try to copy that writing style in your own legal writing. In fact, most of the time you should run as far and as fast as possible away from that writing style.

This isn't because court opinions are poorly written, although some of them are, but because they are written in a different style than you'll be using, and they're written for a different audience than the one you will be addressing. Courts often write opinions with an eye to persuading other judges to rule the same way. That is a very different kind of persuading than the style lawyers adopt when writing to persuade courts. No doubt you'll discuss this at length in your legal writing classes, but for now remember that you are not a judge and you are not writing judicial opinions. Just as you wouldn't adopt the literary style of, say, Stephen King when writing a children's book, so you shouldn't adopt the literary style used by judges when you write as a lawyer.

1. Surface Detail

The first step in becoming an active reader is to get as much surface information from the text as possible. This is information you might otherwise ignore or at best glance at in passing. But there can be a lot of useful and thought-provoking material here just waiting for you pick up and examine.

Following is just the caption—the bibliographical information that appears at the beginning of every court opinion—for a very famous case, read by almost all first-year law students in their first semester as part of a torts course. As you will see, there is a lot of information embedded into this caption, and much of it goes unnoticed by many students. Try to learn as much about the case as you can from this caption before looking at the following text.

PALSGRAF

v.

LONG ISLAND R. CO.

Argued, February 24, 1928
Decided, May 29, 1928.

248 N.Y. 339, 162 N.E. 99

Appeal from a judgment of the Appellate Division of the Supreme Court in the second judicial department, entered December 16, 1927, affirming a judgment in favor of plaintiff entered upon a verdict. Judgment of Appellate Division reversed and complaint dismissed.

CARDOZO, C.J. POUND, LEHMAN and KELLOGG, JJ., concur with CARDOZO, Ch. J.; ANDREWS, J., dissents in opinion in which CRANE and O'BRIEN, JJ., concur.

a. Jurisdiction

The first thing we learn from this caption is that this is a state court decision. You might not know this as a matter of course, but in law school you are required to have a citation manual—usually the *Bluebook* or the *ALWD Manual*—where you can find this information. These books are often thought of only as citation manuals, and that is their principal function. But to do that job, they have to give you comprehensive information about the U.S. court system, and that's helpful for you when you're trying to decide what jurisdiction an opinion comes from. When you look at the section on United States Jurisdictions and look up New York, you'll see that the court that publishes opinions in in the "N.Y." reporter is the and you'll learn that the Court of Appeals of New York is the highest court in the state. That means that this is a state (not federal) court decision. As a rough guide, if there's a state designation somewhere in the citation, then you're probably looking at a state case. If there's an "F." or "Fed." in the citation, the case is probably from federal court. If there is a "U.S." in the citation, the case is probably from the highest federal court, the Supreme Court of the United States.

b. Citation

The caption also gives you the information that can help you find the case if you want to look it up in its complete version. Law school textbooks often excerpt portions of the decisions they include to make the books manageable to read. So they take all the important information for the point they are looking to make and leave the rest out. That can create a misleading impression that all cases revolve around one issue of law—most appellate decision analyze multiple issues—but it does make your textbooks a little shorter and less expensive (law school textbooks are neither short nor cheap—it's all a matter of perspective).

For many reasons, you might want to look at the case in its original form, and you can find it easily based on some of the citation information in the caption, in the line that reads "248 N.Y. 339, 162 N.E. 99." Here's what that means. Legal citations for cases are always in the same format: volume number, volume, and first page number on which the case appears. There might be additional information—for example, the page number on which the specific language you're reading appears, but you should always get the basic information of volume number, reporter (as the books containing court opinions are called), and first page, in that order.

Here, there are two citations because the case appears in two different reporters. The "N.Y." stands for *New York Reports*, the official reporter published by the New York court system. The "N.E." stands for the *North Eastern Reporter*, part of a series of regional reporters published by the West Company, a private commercial publisher. Now isn't the time for a lengthy discussion about the merits of official versus unofficial reporters. For now, you should know that citation manuals have some specific rules about how (and whether) to cite to cases in reporters, but lawyers and judges tend to accept citations to either official or unofficial reporters. Materials found exclusively on electronic databases are a different matter. Most law libraries in the country will have at least one set of all the West Company regional reporters, but if you're looking for the text of the *Palsgraf* opinion, only the largest libraries outside of New York state will also have the *New York Reports* volumes. Most law libraries in New York, however, should have both sets of reporters. Of course, all the decisions in these reporters can be found online at Westlaw, West's online database, or

LexisNexis, its most significant commercial rival. There are many other on-line sources where you can find cases, some of them commercial, for-profit sites that will charge you to access information and some of them free sites that provide information without charge. There are significant advantages and disadvantages to online legal databases, free or commercial, and you will talk about these issues when you study legal research.

c. Finding the Case

Once you've decided which reporter you are going to use, you can go to the library, locate the shelves that contain either the *New York Reports* or the *North Eastern Reporter*, go the particular volume (volume 248 of the *New York Reports* or 162 of the *North Eastern Reporter*) and go to the relevant page. The *Palsgraf* opinion should be there in front of you. But beware, because there's a trap that can catch you. By convention, legal reporter volume numbers are limited to three digits, so when a reporter gets to volume 999, the next volume is not 1,000, but rather is 1. To avoid complete confusion, that book becomes the first volume of the next series of the reporter. That's happened with the *North Eastern Reporter*, so you'll find 162 N.E. and 162 N.E.2d on the shelves. Some reporters, like West's *Pacific Reporter*, are into their third series, so you'll see volumes with P., P.2d, or P.3d on the shelves. Once you're doing a lot of research you'll develop a sensitivity for this, and you'll know there's something wrong if you're looking for a 2005 case in P. or a 1914 case in P.3d. Until then, try to be careful with your notes, and if you look for a case in what appears to be the correct volume and don't find it, remember that you might be looking in the wrong series.

d. Level of Court

It's not just volume numbers that can confuse you. Court names don't al-ways correspond to expectations either. We all know that the Supreme Court—to use its informal name—is the highest court in the federal court system, but that's not always true in the state courts. In a confusing rhetorical twist, the New York trial court system—the lowest of the three-level court system in the state—is known as the "Supreme Court," and the highest court is known as the "Court of Appeals," the name reserved for the intermediate federal court sys-tem. You can see this and the intermediate appellate court's name in the *Pals-graf* caption when you look at the sentence describing how the case got to the Court of Appeals. This case was an appeal from the Appellate Division of the Supreme Court, which tells you that the present decision comes from the sec-ond appellate court to look at the case.

e. Procedural Posture

You know that the case went to verdict in the trial court, because the Appellate Division affirmed a judgment "entered upon a verdict." That doesn't necessarily mean that a jury decided the case—a trial judge can sit as the finder of fact as well as law, and therefore not need a jury to issue a verdict—but it does mean that the case went to trial and went all the way to the end of the trial. So this probably is not a case that was decided just on the law, because those are typically disposed of by motions before putting the parties (and the courts) to the time and expense of a trial.

The plaintiff won both at trial and at the intermediate appellate level. There was a "judgment in favor of plaintiff" at the trial court, and that judgment was affirmed by the Appellate Division on December 16, 1927. But the plaintiff lost in the opinion you are about to read, because the judgment of the Appellate Division was reversed and the complaint was dismissed.

That is important information. It suggests (and we haven't read the decision yet, so we can't be sure about this) that this opinion reveals something new about the law because the Court of Appeals is saying that this case never should have made it out of the starting blocks—the complaint was dismissed, which is something that normally happens very early in the judicial process. It often means that the plaintiff has not stated a cause of action on which relief can be granted, and because most lawyers and judges know what causes of action are and are not available to plaintiffs, it seems unlikely that they knew in this case that the plaintiff's cause of action wasn't viable. If they're learning that now for the first time, it means that the Court of Appeals is saying something new, making this an important case in the development of the law in this area.

f. Existence of a Dissent

We can see already in the caption that whatever this court is saying, it isn't speaking with a completely unified voice. In fact, seven judges are identified in the caption, and only four of them—Cardozo, Pound, Lehmann, and Kellogg—were in the majority. Judges Andrews, Crane, and O'Brien dissented from the majority's opinion, and Judge Andrews wrote a dissenting opinion. Dissents are valuable things for law students, because often your teachers will want you to take the other side of a decision to see how flexible your thinking is, and the dissenting opinion often presents other viewpoints that will help you test the majority opinion and the way you think about it. Frequently, times have changed since the court's decision was published, and what was once a dissent might now be the law. In short, you should be happy when you see a majority decision with a dissenting opinion; you'll have a lot more to work with as you prepare for class.

g. Date of Decision

Another vital piece of information that's often completely overlooked by law students and lawyers is the date of the case. The *Palsgraf* decision was published in 1928, more than 80 years ago. A lot has changed in the United States since then — this was the year before the Wall Street crash that brought on the Great Depression, 14 years before the nation joined World War II, and less than a year after the release of *The Jazz Singer*, the first talking movie, in October 1927. So the country was a very different place; maybe this decision is no longer good law as the result of the legal and societal changes that have occurred. Even if the law announced in the decision hasn't been overturned, it is possible that the court's rationale for reaching its decision is outdated, and that might cause you to suspect the continued vitality of the decision. You should always look at the date of a decision and make careful note of it.

For lawyers experienced in the delays inherent in contemporary practice, the dates of the Appellate Division's decision, the hearing in the Court of Appeals, and the Court of Appeals's decision might bring a wry smile. The intermediate appellate court's decision was handed down on December 16, 1927, and the case was heard by the Court of Appeals just over two months later — an astonishingly short time to lawyers today. Even more astonishingly, the Court of Appeals handed down its decision just three months after that. So from verdict to final resolution by the Court of Appeals (not counting a motion for reconsideration, which was decided very quickly as well) took only five months. If the case was being heard today, it likely would have taken three or more years to move through the system to reach the point identified in the opinion.

h. Identity of the Judge Who Wrote the Opinion

Finally, we know the identity of the judge who wrote this decision, Chief Judge (that's what the "C.J." initials stand for) Cardozo. Often, the identity of the judge who writes an opinion doesn't have much historical significance; it's something the parties in a pending case want to know so they can tailor their arguments to a particular judge's judicial philosophy, if possible, but there have been many judges on the New York Court of Appeals who have not made much of a historical mark.

Judge Cardozo isn't one of them. He's one of the towering figures of American jurisprudence in the first part of the twentieth century and even has a law school named after him — the Benjamin N. Cardozo Law School, located on

Fifth Avenue in Greenwich Village, New York City. A quick Google search reveals how important a figure Judge Cardozo was to the law, suggesting that any decision he wrote is not to be taken lightly, and any decision of his chosen by the editors of a law school textbook is particularly important.

It's true, of course, that any opinion included in a law school textbook is, by definition, important to you. The selection of a Cardozo case (and there are other judges, some even older than Cardozo and some more contemporary than him, that are similarly important in the development of the law) means that this is a particularly significant case. That doesn't mean that you will agree with the decision reached by Judge Cardozo, or even that it is still good law today, but it means that you need to pay close attention to this case.

This is a lot of information to be drawn from one short caption. You couldn't be expected to learn all of it before coming to law school, of course, and some of this information might only reveal itself to you after a year or so of legal study. Whenever you find something to which you don't know the answer ("what does it mean that the court says the complaint is dismissed?"), you should make a note to learn the answer, either in class or by yourself. Knowing what you don't know and figuring out how to learn the answer is one of the most valuable skills you can learn in law school.

2. Reading Like a Lawyer

Let's continue with the *Palsgraf* case and read the facts as the court wrote them to see what we can glean. I'm not going to talk about the legal importance of the case or why so many law students read about it; that's something best handled by your torts professor. Reading the facts can help demonstrate the active reading process and the sort of questions you might be asking yourself as you read cases and brief cases in preparation for class.

Here are the facts of one of the most famous cases in U.S. jurisprudence. I include the text twice; once just as it appears in the court's decision, and once with the questions one might ask the text if one was preparing for class.

> Plaintiff was standing on a platform of defendant's railroad after buying a ticket to go to Rockaway Beach. A train stopped at the station, bound for another place. Two men ran forward to catch it. One of the men reached the platform of the car without mishap, though the train was already moving. The other man, carrying a package, jumped aboard the car, but seemed unsteady as if about to fall. A guard on the car, who had held the door open, reached forward to help him in, and another guard on the platform pushed him from behind. In this

act, the package was dislodged, and fell upon the rails. It was a package of small size, about fifteen inches long, and was covered by a newspaper. In fact it contained fireworks, but there was nothing in its appearance to give notice of its contents. The fireworks when they fell exploded. The shock of the explosion threw down some scales at the other end of the platform, many feet away. The scales struck the plaintiff, causing injuries for which she sues.

This is a very economical piece of writing, crafted with great care. The writing is leaner and clearer than many of the judicial opinions you'll read. The facts also suggest that Judge Cardozo was writing more of an advocacy piece than you might normally expect in a judicial opinion; this reads more like a set of facts you would find in a document filed by a lawyer to persuade a court of something rather than something written by a judge who (one would think) doesn't have to persuade readers of anything. To illustrate that, and to see how you might go about gleaning information from this text, let's read this again, this time with some questions and comments. Before you read the questions though, you might want to go back over the unedited version of the *Palsgraf* facts and make a note of your own questions. Then read my questions and compare them to your own. Are they the same? Did we focus on the same areas or on completely different things? In retrospect, do you prefer your approach to mine or vice versa?

Plaintiff was standing on a platform of defendant's railroad after buying a ticket to go to Rockaway Beach. [Where was she standing? Was she at the edge of the platform, or was she up against the wall?] **A train stopped at the station, bound for another place.** [Was this train on the line closest to the platform where the plaintiff was standing, or was it on another line? In other words, was this train coming down the same tracks as the train the plaintiff was waiting for, or was it in a different part of the station? Why isn't the judge telling us how close the plaintiff was to this train? Is that going to be important, or doesn't it matter?] **Two men ran forward to catch it. One of the men reached the platform of the car without mishap, though the train was already moving.** [If this man reached the train without mishap, why are we reading about him? Presumably the second man had the problem, so why did the judge tell us about this first man? He seems irrelevant. Was there only one car to this train? The opinion says "the car," implying that there was only one, but we don't know that for sure. Does this matter?] **The other man, carrying a package, jumped aboard the car, but seemed unsteady as if about to fall. A guard on the car, who had held the door open, reached forward to help him in, and another guard**

on the platform pushed him from behind. [Would it have made a difference if the first man who jumped onto the train had tried to help this man? Suppose a passenger on the platform, instead of a guard, had pushed the man from behind? Presumably the guards are both employees of the railroad, making them agents of the railroad. Will that make a difference?] **In this act, the package was dislodged, and fell upon the rails. It was a package of small size, about fifteen inches long, and was covered by a newspaper.** [The judge says the package was small in size and then gives us the dimensions, allowing us to form a pretty exact picture of the size of the package. Is it going to be important that it was a small package? Why does he tell us the package was covered in newspaper?] **In fact it contained fireworks, but there was nothing in its appearance to give notice of its contents.** [Maybe he told us it was covered in newspaper so that we would believe him when he said there was nothing to give notice of the contents of the package. He's given us some specific information about that and told us generally that no one could tell what kind of package the man was carrying, so it seems that this is important. There is no obvious reason to emphasize something like this, especially in a document so tightly written, if this wasn't important. Whatever else is going on, it seems that the fact that no one except the man carrying the package could know what was in it is going to be important.] **The fireworks when they fell exploded. The shock of the explosion threw down some scales at the other end of the platform, many feet away.** [How many feet away? The judge gave us specific information about length when it was important to him—the package was small, about 15 inches long. Here he seems to be obscuring the distance the plaintiff was from the explosion. We know she's standing on a platform in the station, but we don't know where on the platform she's standing, and we don't know for sure if she is even on the same platform as the train or on some other platform in the station. Even assuming this is a two-line station, that could make a big difference in the proximity of the woman to the explosion. Why does the judge give us both general and specific information sometimes (the size of the package, the fact that no one could know what was in the package because it was covered in newspaper) and general information at other times (how far away from the explosion the woman was)?] **The scales struck the plaintiff, causing injuries for which she sues.** [He doesn't say that the scales were dislodged by the explosion, but that seems to be implied by all of this. What kind of scales—wall-mounted or standing on the floor?

Does it matter? Was she standing close to the scales, or did they fly through the air before they hit her? The judge does not tell us how badly she was injured, so we can guess that isn't going to be important to the court's decision.]

The important thing here is that you ask questions during the reading process and think and reflect on what the text is saying, what it's not saying, and why the writer has chosen to give some information and seems to be withholding other information. In the *Palsgraf* case, for instance, do we believe that Judge Cardozo didn't have access to the information about how far away Ms. Palsgraf was from the explosion? Or does it seem more likely that if he knew the dimensions of the package the man was carrying, he probably knew about how far away she was? Why is he not telling us something and is content instead to use the general phrase "the other end of the platform, many feet away." How far is "many" feet? Does "the other end of the platform" mean that she was at one end, or does it just mean that she wasn't right beside the explosion? It could be, of course, that the parties didn't give the court this information. At this point in the reading we don't know. The important thing is to raise the question, not necessarily to know the answer.

This ambiguity is in stark contrast to the specific information we get in other parts of the fact statement. For instance, we learn how many men were running for the train; even though we don't seem to need to know anything about the second man, we learn that the package was small and precisely what size it was, and we learn why no one could tell what was in it. Yet throughout the statement of facts, we're left without a clear sense of where Ms. Palsgraf is standing in relation to the scales, the train, or the explosion. Because she's the litigant in this case, surely that would be helpful information for us to have.

Maybe this fact is important, and maybe it isn't. The only way to know for sure is to read the rest of the decision and then discuss it in class with your professor and your colleagues. You will see that I often asked whether a question or series of questions mattered at all. The only way to answer that is to read the rest of the text with those questions firmly in mind. Now you have some questions to ask the rest of the text, and that's a much better position to be in than just reading the opinion passively, hoping that everything will become clear at the end.

Are these the only questions we might ask about the information contained in the statement of facts? Probably not; there are other questions we might want to ask about the style of writing. How has the judge written this fact statement—using long, flowing sentences full of flowery rhetoric and long words, or in short, clear, sentences? In fact, the language is very simple, and the sentences are so short they border on terse. Is this the style of someone who is trying to hide something or someone who is trying very hard to be seen as giving credible, accurate information? If the judge is trying to be clear and informative, why does he seemingly obscure some of the information? Or is that a mistaken impression?

Once you've thought about all of these things, try to predict what's going to happen before reading any further. Based on what you've read, and without any knowledge of the rest of the court's decision, do you think Ms. Palsgraf won or lost her suit against the railroad company? Why? What about the way the facts are written leads you to that impression?

Because this is a book about things you can do before you come to law school and not a torts textbook, I will leave the rest of the *Palsgraf* case to your torts class. If you've read the facts as carefully as possible and asked yourself a good series of questions about the case, you will remember a lot about it when it comes up in class, and you'll have an interesting time talking about its facts and its legal implications.

For present purposes, you can see that a lot of things are going on in what seems like (at a superficial reading) a very simple and clear set of facts. It's like this—or should be, at any rate—with almost everything you read. Don't just look at what information you're given and think about what information you don't have. Try to think why it might be that you are told some things and not others. Think about *how* you're told. Is the writer trying to persuade you of something by virtue of the style of writing, the words chosen, the way the words are organized, and so on?

Reading like this takes a lot of time and effort, but it is repaid by a much deeper understanding of what is really going on in the text and how the writer is trying to communicate. Once you understand those two things, you not only understand the law to a much greater degree than you will as a superficial and passive reader of information, you also better understand the writing techniques you have to employ to persuade readers of your work to accept those propositions you want them to accept, making you a more effective legal communicator. If all this seems a little daunting, don't worry: the process gets easier each time you read a case and will soon be second nature to you if you work at it.

> **Exercise:** As you practice active reading, make notes of the questions you have. Think about what you're being told, what you're not being told, and how the writer has opted to tell you information. Expand your reading to include nonjournalistic pieces as well, fictional and nonfiction. Look for the gaps in information and try to see how the writer covers over any weak spots. Try to predict what's coming in the next section

or the next chapter. If you're right, congratulate yourself. If not, think about what you might have missed or whether the writer was intentionally trying to deceive you. Of course, the writer could also be incompetent. If you decide that was the problem, discard that writer's work and find someone else to read. If you conclude that you missed something, vow not to be fooled again and start the process over again.

C. Reading and the Internet

The general perception of those who study these things is that reading is in trouble in this country. Recent surveys suggest that current generations are reading significantly less than did previous generations, and reading seems to be a less important activity than it used to be.

The reasons behind these statistics are unknown, but there is no arguing that the Internet has risen from a limited phenomenon known to very few people in 1988 to the ubiquitous daily presence it is today. It's hard to argue that the Internet hasn't had at least some impact on the way we receive and process written information. It's certainly true that any changes the Internet has had on reading habits are not yet reflected in most law school curricula. You will be expected to read and process information from books in the same way as those who were in law school before the Internet. That means you might have to work harder to acquire or reacquire reading skills you might not have learned or that might have atrophied. The good news is that there is a well-recognized approach that will help you read your law school texts in as active a manner as possible. We talk about that next.

4

Case Briefing

Imagine that there's a system that automates the active reading process, so that you analyze and absorb the important information from everything you read for your law school classes. This system will help you learn how to read actively, and eventually that process will become second nature to you. It will also help you prepare for class. If you take this system seriously and work at it every day, your law school grades will surely be higher than if you only adopt it half-heartedly or not at all. And the really wonderful thing is that no matter how much they're told about it, and no matter how much they're told how beneficial to them this system will be, almost all of your law school colleagues will either ignore it completely or, at best, will work at it for a month or so and then give it up, leaving you as one of the few people to benefit from it. It's a huge advantage for you if you are one of the few to take it seriously.

Such a system exists, of course, and as careful readers of texts, you have figured out that it's the *case brief*. The law uses words differently than the rest of the English-speaking world, and sometimes lawyers use the same word to mean different things. So it is with *brief*. You might think of the word as synonymous with *short*, and that probably is the derivation of its legal meaning. In this context at least, the case *brief* is actually a series of notes about a case that follows a predetermined format so that you take down the same information, in the same order, about every case you read.

The case brief is a very well-established facet of the first year in law school, and perhaps that explains why so few students take it seriously. Here is the typical trajectory of a law student's involvement with the case brief: the student reads about case briefs over the summer and comes to law school filled with good intentions about preparing a brief for every case. The student comes to school, hears all the first-year teachers talking about how important briefing is, and vows to follow through on the summer's good intentions. The student talks to other law students—especially upper-class ones—and hears that no one keeps briefing cases after a month or so. The student discovers (1) that briefing takes time, and (2) that commercial or "canned" briefs are published for each course, often keyed right to the particular textbook used to study torts, or contracts, or some other subject. The student buys a book of canned briefs, decides that they will suffice to keep the student safe when called on by the teacher in class, and, at best, resorts to making marginal notes about cases in the textbook.

I am under no illusions: many (perhaps most) of you will behave this way, even though I live in hope. We all tend to take the path of least resistance to achieve a goal, and there's no doubt that—viewed one way—a book of canned briefs is easier to acquire than a semester's worth of personally prepared briefs that accompany the cases in a particular subject. It's also true that reading the canned briefs for a class will take substantially less time than preparing the briefs yourself. Very few of you came to law school expecting it to be easy, however, and most of you assumed that class preparation was going to take a substantial amount of time. If you can remember that in the middle of the semester, when things are getting hectic and you have writing assignments and complex class preparation vying for your time, and if you can force yourself to put in the time necessary to do a complete job preparing for class every day, your grades will surely be higher than if you succumb to the temptation of relying on canned briefs.

The reason for this should be obvious by now. Although briefs are often talked about as though they were developed solely for the purpose of helping you answer all the awkward questions a professor might ask you during a Socratic question-and-answer session during class (and they are very helpful in preparing you for the questions that might come at you during such a session), their real value is in helping you have a Socratic session with *yourself*. You ask yourself questions about the case as you're reading it, and then record your answers. By going through that process, checking your responses with what your teacher expects you to learn from the case, and then refining your questions and answers for the next set of cases you read, and repeating this throughout the semester and the rest of law school, you will discover that you have learned how to teach yourself about the law. That's perhaps the most important skill you can learn in school.

Maybe all the case brief needs is better spin. Instead of thinking of the case brief as a panic avoidance mechanism for those times when you're called on in class, think of it instead as a key that unlocks the mysteries of law school and makes you a better, more analytical reader. That's a skill that will help you get better grades, get a better job after law school, and make you a better, more successful lawyer. Not a bad return for the investment of a little time.

A. How to Brief

The great thing about case briefs is that they are relatively easy to construct, and even though they might take a while to prepare at first, you'll get better and faster with more practice. Let's go through the process now. Later in this section, I include a general template you can use to start practicing case briefs. As you will learn, though, the best case brief is one that gives you the information you need when you need it, so you should feel free to modify this template to suit your own needs.

There is a very key caveat to keep in mind at this point: this is my idea of what makes a good brief. Your professors might want you to record different information, and each professor might have a completely different idea of what makes a good brief. Your job is to keep your professors happy, so brief cases for that professor's class in the way that professor tells you. It's no good telling Professor A that Professor B told you to brief cases differently—Professor A won't care, and you'll suffer as a result. If one or more of your professors tells you to do things differently than what I outline here, go with what your professor tells you. You will never go wrong doing what your professor tells you to do!

With that in mind, here's a quick description of the important elements of a brief.

1. Read the Case First

Paradoxically, my first piece of advice on how to brief a case is to *not* brief the case right away. Rather than starting in with drafting a brief, the first thing you should do is to read through the case to find out what it's about, what the legal issues involved might be, and how the case comes out.

Reading the case before you brief it helps orient you to the terrain of the case; it's a scouting mission to prepare you for what's coming. Careful litigators will tell you that they look around a courtroom before the trial begins, just to get a sense of the room: how the lighting and acoustics in the room might affect their presentations; how the placement of tables and chairs might affect their movement around the courtroom; how many electrical outlets there are and how that might affect the number and type of presentation devices they might use; and so on. That reconnoitering before the real work begins is sensible planning on their part, and it is for you as well. Reading through a case orients you to the essential issues at stake and gets your brain into gear, so when you come back to the beginning to start the briefing process, you will already have questions ready to ask the text.

2. *Case Title and Citation*

The first thing a written brief should contain is obvious—you need to record the case name and where you read it so you can find it again if you need to check on something. Write down all the relevant bibliographical information—the case name, the date it was decided, the court that decided the case, and (if you're reading the case in one of your textbooks) the page in the textbook where the case begins.

All of this (except for the textbook page) is information typically found in a case citation. If your textbook gives you the citation information, record it accurately, but try to do more than just write that information down. Think about it: what court decided this case? Does that mean it's a federal or state court? Might there be an appeal from this decision? Where would that appeal be filed and how (certiorari or appeal of right)? On whom is this decision binding? When was this decision handed down by the court? Does the date mean that this is likely to still be good law or might this decision have been overruled? And so on. The more information you can extract from every part of the case, the better off you will be.

Don't worry if you can't come up with answers to all of these questions yet. Keep asking them, and recording what you know (and what you don't know). If your teacher flags one of your unanswered questions in class, at least you are asking the right questions.

3. *Identity of the Parties*

The names of at least the first plaintiff—or the governmental entity prosecuting the case in a criminal case—and the first defendant listed on the complaint are given as part of the title of the case. You can learn some things from looking at the names and any other explanatory information given in the case name. For example, most cases that have the "United States of America" or "State of ___" as one of the parties are probably criminal cases. Any case that includes the words "on behalf of him (or her) self and all other similarly situated" after a party's name is probably a class action. Any case in which one of the parties is a thing—"United States v. the Motor Cruiser 'Drug Runner,'" for example—is probably a case proceeding *in rem*. If that doesn't mean anything to you yet, that's okay, but look up the term in a legal dictionary so you can learn what it means.

One thing that you cannot always be sure of from the party names is who is the plaintiff (in a civil case) and who is the defendant. As a general rule, the party invoking the court's jurisdiction comes on the left side of the "v." and the party who doesn't want to be in front of the court is on the right. That means that in civil trial court captions, the plaintiff is on the left of the v., and the defendant is on the right.

The cases you tend to read in law school are usually from appellate courts, and case names sometimes change when they get to that stage. Some courts will keep the order of names the same as they were at trial, whereas others will flip the names around if the defendant lost at the lower level and is now appealing the decision (and, therefore, is the one invoking the appellate court's jurisdiction). Sometimes a case lasts so long that one or more of the parties drops out and is replaced by another party; that happens often in cases heard by the Supreme Court.

Even if the names and their order don't change, the legal relationship between the parties changes based on where the case is in the judicial process. At a trial of a civil case, for instance, there's a plaintiff and a defendant (in criminal cases there's no plaintiff, it's usually either "the state" or "the United States." There is still a defendant). On appeal, there's an appellant (the party bringing the appeal) and an appellee. You can't tell whether the appellant was the plaintiff or the defendant at trial; it depends on who won and who lost at the trial court stage. Some courts call the party by both names—"John Smith, defendant/appellant" for example—and others don't. If a party has persuaded the U.S. Supreme Court (or another court where a petition for certiorari was necessary) to hear a case, then that party is properly known as *petitioner* and the other side is the *respondent*.

It should be no surprise for you that people—even lawyers and judges— can get very confused by all of this. When the same person can be a plaintiff, an appellee, and a petitioner, things can get hopelessly muddled. That's not even to consider the not-unusual situation of what happens when one or other of the named parties has dropped out of the case before it reaches the Supreme Court. There are two things you can do to keep organized. First, your brief should be meticulous and consistent in the way it refers to everyone involved in the case. Second, it usually helps to refer to people by their name, rather than their legal relationship. Sometimes you can't follow this second piece of advice because your professor might want to be sure that you know the difference between a plaintiff, a defendant, an appellant, an appellee, a petitioner, and a respondent. You will usually know when your professor wants that kind of detail. Most of the time, though, you are better off sticking to names.

4. Procedural History

The procedural history of a case is an important detail, although it's not always possible to understand how the case got to where it was when the opinion was written. That's because many of the cases in your textbooks are heavily edited to keep your books down to a manageable size. If the editor didn't feel that the procedural history of a particular case was important, it might well have been cut, although it will probably be in the original version of the court's opinion.

Understanding the procedural posture of a case is a good way to be sure you understand where the case is now. You might be reading a trial court's decision regarding a summary judgment motion filed by one of the parties. That usually (remember, there aren't many absolutes in the law) means that the discovery process is over but the case has not yet reached trial. You might be reading a trial court's decision concerning a suppression motion in a criminal case, meaning that the case definitely hasn't gone to trial. You might be reading an interlocutory appeal, and if you are, you should look up *interlocutory* in a legal dictionary so you understand what it means and what it says about the procedural posture of a case. You might be reading a Supreme Court decision, in which case you should try to understand where the case came from and what that says about the legal issues before the Court.

5. *Facts*

The facts are an absolutely essential part of understanding a case. Facts are so important to us as lawyers, in fact, that some of us joke that you should come to fact school instead of law school. This joke points out the central role the facts play in almost any given case. A lawyer's skill is measured not so much in the ability to find law but more in how well he or she can analogize and distinguish the facts of one case from another.

You will find that dynamic playing out in law school classes almost from the beginning. Your professors might ask you to assume that the court ruled as it did in a particular case but then assume that a fact has changed. They will ask you how that changed fact might affect the outcome of the case. They might change another fact, and another, and so on. Each time the facts change, you are being asked to explore how well you understand the doctrinal underpinning of the court's decision and the inextricable relationship of fact and law that make the common law endlessly fascinating for students and lawyers alike.

You won't be able to cope with this type of exercise if you don't understand the facts of the case as written, so this is your chance to note down the salient facts of the case. The court already selected these for you by recording them. The facts you read in a court opinion aren't the only ones that were established at trial and probably aren't the same facts that the parties identified as being important in their briefs. They are the facts that the court felt to be important when it wrote its opinion, and that's a gift for you because it means there aren't too many facts for you to write down.

Even so, you don't have to write all the facts down; in fact, you shouldn't even try to do that—you would just be copying the court's facts section word for word. Rather, you should write only those facts necessary to trigger your memory so that you can reproduce the legally relevant facts of the case if asked, either by your professor, in class, or by yourself when you're preparing for exams. Your facts might be in note form or in complete sentences. It doesn't matter; there aren't any style points available for briefs, and probably no one but you will ever see the document you are preparing. You can use whatever abbreviations and strange marks you want. The only thing that matters is that you can reproduce the facts coherently when necessary.

You need to be able to reproduce the facts accurately as well as coherently. There's no point thinking that Ms. Palsgraf wasn't injured by some falling scales when, in fact, she *was* injured. As you're drafting the facts section of your brief, be careful to make sure that you can not only reproduce the facts of the case but also reproduce them accurately. You might be surprised at how difficult this is—our memories are not nearly as infallible as we would like to think— and you will get better with practice.

6. Issues

When we talk about issues, we start getting into the legal core of the case. The issue is the legal question that the court has to address to dispose of the case. Courts often tell you the issue in a sentence that looks something like this: "In this case, we are asked to address the issue of ...", or even "The issue in this case is ..." Those are opinions you'll come to cherish, because they often make your life simpler.

When you are framing the issue, be sure you do it in a way that actually helps you describe what's happening in the case. This isn't always as simple as it sounds. The issue in every case, when reduced to its fundamentals, is whether the plaintiff wins, but framing the issue in that way doesn't give you any insight into the legal issues at stake. A better issue statement is one that articulates the legal principle the court is addressing and the conflict between the parties on that principle. So a better issue statement might read "Whether defendant owed plaintiff a duty of care, where the harm plaintiff suffered was not foreseeable from defendant's actions." Not perfect perhaps, but at least more informative than "does plaintiff win?"

It's important—crucial, really—that you understand a case well enough to be able to express the issue raised in your own words. If you can do that, you are probably in control of the material. If you can't, you haven't read the case carefully enough and you need to go back and do some work on it. This is one of the reasons that canned briefs are no help to you—they disengage you from the material. They might give you an issue statement, summarized from the case, that will work if you're called on in class, but just repeating it to your professor doesn't mean you understand it. The only true guarantee that you will understand the issues involved in a case is to grapple with the opinion until you can generate your own statement of the issue.

7. *Summary of Arguments*

This can be tricky, because courts don't always tell you what the parties argued. Rather, they might discuss the issues raised and how they dealt with them. If the court tells you that one of the parties raised an argument, make a note of it. Understanding the arguments the parties made, and the order in which they raised them, can help you understand the way the lawyers thought about the case—often, that's very different from the way the court thinks about the case. Your professor might well ask what you thought of a particular argument and how you might have refined it to produce a different result. As you notate the arguments made by the parties, think about whether they are good arguments and how you would have framed things if you had been one of the lawyers on the case.

8. *Holding*

The *holding* of a case is the rule of law expressed by the court as a result of its analysis of the facts and law. The holding is different from the *result*, which is merely a statement of who wins. The holding of the case contains the rule of law necessary to reach that result.

If the issue statement is "whether defendant owed plaintiff a duty of care, where the harm plaintiff suffered was not foreseeable from defendant's actions," we can see that "no" is not an adequate description of the holding. A better summary would be "No. Just because the defendant was negligent toward one party does not mean that the defendant was negligent toward the plaintiff. Negligence depends on the relationship between the parties, which must be found in the foreseeability of harm to the person injured." Again, perhaps this is not the most elegantly phrased holding you will ever read, but at least it is relatively informative.

9. *Court's Rationale for Holding*

Knowing what the court was asked to decide and how it actually decided it are crucial details, but perhaps the most important thing to understand is *why* the court ruled as it did. This rationale—which almost all courts will give to explain the holding—gives you an insight into how the court thinks about an issue. Understanding the rationale behind the decision is of the first importance, not only to your performance in class but also to your performance as a lawyer. This is the information that allows you to analogize and distinguish the facts of other cases to this opinion, a critically important skill for lawyers to have.

Courts being courts, you'll discover that there is often an extensive discussion of the rationale behind a decision, and often an even more extensive discussion that isn't relevant to the decision. This is known as *dicta*, which should mean "something we didn't need to say," but is actually from the Latin for "to say." So dicta is language that was not necessary for the court to reach its disposition of the case but that it felt like throwing into the opinion. It's important for you to be able to distinguish the holding, the language explaining the rationale behind the holding, and dicta, which doesn't have any direct bearing on the holding, because dicta has no binding effect on future decisions. You will often hear a lawyer argue language from a case to a judge only for the judge to say "Yes counsel, but isn't that just dicta?"

So why do courts write dicta in opinions? Is it just because they like to hear the sound of their voices in writing? Well, maybe sometimes. But there is a good and valid reason for dicta; more often than not you'll be happy to see it in an opinion because dicta is often what allows you to answer those "change the facts" questions. Understanding not just the specific reasons the court reached a particular decision but also the more broad reasoning process the court went through often helps us predict how the court might rule if different facts were presented, and that is often very valuable information.

10. *The Court's Order*

Just because you know what the court decided to do and why does not mean you know what the court actually did about its decision. Strangely enough, this is often the least important part of the decision for lawyers and law students, who are looking at the case more for the rules and policies it expresses and not for the action it took, although obviously it's of paramount importance to the litigants and the lawyers who represent them. You should keep a note of the order in the case if the opinion includes it.

The action a court takes in a case is usually included as a terse statement at the end of the opinion — "the defendant's conviction is affirmed," or "plaintiff's motion is denied." Sometimes an appellate court might reverse the trial court, sometimes it might remand the case back to the trial court for further proceedings in light of the opinion, but something always happens — courts are, after all, practical bodies that resolve actual disputes, and that resolution has to be embodied somehow. Making a practice of looking for this resolution (even if your professor doesn't make a habit of asking about it) will give you an insight into the way courts operate as a practical matter ("Why did the court remand this case back to the trial court? Because this decision leaves something still to be done before the case can be finally resolved") and the more things that become second nature to you as you read a court opinion, the better prepared you will be to be a practicing lawyer.

11. Your Thoughts and Comments

You might not think your thoughts and opinions about a case will matter that much, but this is the most important section of the brief in my opinion, because this is where you record your reactions to what the court did, and to do that you have to have read the case in an active manner. As you are reading the case, you should be asking yourself—and the case—questions: Does this make sense? Do I agree with the court when it says? Does this opinion build on what I learned from the cases I've read before, or does it go in a different direction? How would I have resolved this question? Does this seem like a just result? And so on.

The more questions you ask as you read something, the more involved you are with the text and with the court's thinking as it explains what it did. When this works properly, it's as if you are having a dialogue with the court—the same dialogue you have in class as you go through the case. There is no better way to prepare for class than to ask yourself all the questions your professor is going to ask about the case and think carefully about the answers as you read the case at home or in the library.

When I say you should ask the case questions, you should feel uninhibited about actually asking those questions out loud—literally talking to the text. Avoid giving others the impression that you're conducting an internal conversation with yourself, because they might misinterpret what's going on and think that the pressure of law school has become too much for you. If you are going to talk out loud to the text (and I do, all the time—especially when I'm grading writing assignments), you might want to do it in a place where no one can hear you. If you can't talk to the text in a place where no one can hear you, you might have to talk using your mind rather than your voice. Even if you have to do it silently, I encourage you to have a conscious conversation with the text. Think of it as a rehearsal for class, with you reading the professor's lines as well as your own.

B. Briefing in Action

How does the briefing process work in action? It's impossible for me to show you the conversation I would have with a text, of course, but I can show you a brief I have prepared for a short case and include some of the questions and comments I had for the text. If you would like to practice your briefing skills, a never-ending stream of opinions is available to you. Find a website for one of the many state or federal appellate courts, and you'll find that the court has posted its decisions right on the site, available to anyone who wants to read them. Look for decisions that are relatively short (no more than five pages long), print them out, and start briefing.

Between now and when you come to law school, try to brief one case a day (no more—you have to do other things over the summer). If you do that, you'll be in very good shape to start learning as soon as you come to school.

For now, though, read the following case and try your hand at briefing it first, then read through my brief. Don't worry about not knowing anything about the law of this particular area; I had never heard of the statute the court construes here either, although I knew there had to be something somewhere that states the content of this statute. Try to get as much as you can from the case and that will be a good start.

I include a template to help you organize your brief. Feel free to move the order around, rename the sections, do anything you want to make the briefs you generate useful to you. Keep your format consistent once you have hit on something that works for you. One of the most valuable things about a brief is that it can give you the information you're looking for in exactly the same place each time. If you're under pressure in class, you'll know exactly where to look to get the information necessary to answer a tricky question.

Let's read about Mr. Rippee's really bad New Year's celebration in 1991 and see what we can learn about the mistake he made.

United States Court of Appeals, Seventh Circuit.

UNITED STATES of America, Plaintiff-Appellee,

v.

Robert J. RIPPEE, Defendant-Appellant.

No. 91-2485.

Argued Dec. 2, 1991.
Decided April 14, 1992.

Defendant was convicted in the United States District Court for the Southern District of Illinois, William D. Stiehl, J., of impersonating a federal officer and he appealed. The Court of Appeals, Manion, Circuit Judge, held that defendant who avoided a traffic ticket as a result of his false personation of a United States marshal obtained something of value and thus could be convicted.

Affirmed.

MANION, Circuit Judge.

By pretending to be a United States Marshal, Robert J. Rippee talked his way out of a traffic ticket and into an indictment in federal court. A jury convicted Rippee of impersonating a federal officer to obtain a thing of value in violation of 18 U.S.C. §912 (1976), and the district judge sentenced Rippee to seven months imprisonment pursuant to the Sentencing Guidelines. On appeal, Rippee argues only that the district court erred in denying his motion to dismiss the indictment for failure to state an offense under section 912. We affirm the defendant's conviction.

I. Background

A. Facts

On January 1, 1991, officers from the National City, Illinois, Police Department stopped Rippee for making an illegal U-turn. The officers let Rippee go without a ticket, however, when he told them he was a United States Marshal on his way to break up a fight at Fannies' Night Club in Brooklyn, Illinois.

On February 21, 1991, the grand jury in the Southern District of Illinois charged Rippee in a one-count indictment with obtaining a thing of value by pretending to be an officer acting under the authority of the United States in violation of 18 U.S.C. §912. Rippee filed a motion to dismiss the indictment arguing that the indictment failed to state an offense under section 912. After the district court denied the motion, the case proceeded to trial. Rippee stipulated that he was not and had never been a United States Marshal. After hearing the evidence, the jury convicted Rippee.

B. Statute

Since 1948, 18 U.S.C. § 912 has read as follows:

> Whoever falsely assumes or pretends to be an officer or employee acting under the authority of the United States or any department, agency or officer thereof, and acts as such, or in such pretended character demands or obtains any money, paper, document, or thing of value, shall be fined not more than $1000 or imprisoned not more than three years, or both.

Rippee seeks to distinguish his conduct from the conduct criminalized under section 912 in two ways. First, Rippee argues that even though he did impersonate a federal officer he did not "obtain a thing of value." Therefore, his conduct did not fall within the category of conduct prohibited by section 912. Second, Rippee argues, even if he obtained a thing of value, he acted for his personal benefit and not as a representative of the United States, which absolves him from criminal liability under section 912.

II. Analysis

Section 912 criminalizes two kinds of conduct: (1) false impersonation of a federal official coupled with an overt act in conformity with the pretense and (2) false impersonation of a federal official coupled with demanding or obtaining a thing of value. *United States v. Kimberlin,* 781 F.2d 1247, 1250 (7th Cir., 1985), *cert. denied,* 479 U.S. 938 (1986) (citing *United States v. Barnow,* 239 U.S. 74, 75 (1915) (decided under the predecessor statute to § 912). Rippee's indictment charges him with the second type of section 912 offense, and his argument before this court initially requires us to determine what it means to "obtain a thing of value" within the meaning of the statute.

As Rippee correctly observes, most cases under section 912 involve defendants who obtain money, credit or property as a result of deceit. *E.g., Kimberlin,* 781 F.2d at 1249 (defendant used Department of Defense insignia to obtain property); *United States v. Etheridge,* 512 F.2d 1249, 1250 (2d Cir., 1975), *cert. denied,* 423 U.S. 843 (1975) (defendant obtained loan of $200 from Army Emergency Relief by falsely stating that he was a current member of the U.S. Army); *United States v. Milton,* 421 F.2d 586, 587 (10th Cir., 1970) (defendant represented himself as an FBI agent to obtain money); *Honea v. United States,* 344 F.2d 798, 800–801 (5th Cir., 1965) (defendant represented himself as a CIA agent and obtained $4000). The phrase "thing of value" under section 912 has also been construed to encompass more than tangible objects having commercial worth. *United States v. Sheker,* 618 F.2d 607, 609 (9th Cir., 1980) (holding that information constituted a "thing of value"). Rippee observes, however, that "[e]ven those cases which do not involve a literal transfer of cash, credit, or other valuable property still require that the defendant *receive* something for his efforts in order to be convicted" (Appellant's Brief at 3). In Rippee's view, his conduct falls outside the reach of section 912 because he *avoided* something but *obtained* nothing.

Rippee proposes a novel interpretation of section 912, and we have found no indication that any other circuit has pondered the meaning of the word "obtain" in the context of section 912. However, Rippee's semantic distinction between "avoid" and "obtain" in this case fails because Rippee did obtain something of value— forbearance. Forbearance by the National City Police conferred upon Rippee a substantial benefit because if Rippee had received a ticket (instead of forbearance) he may have had to pay a fine, appear in court, and perhaps even shoulder an increase in insurance premiums. Also, as the district court noted, Rippee at least gained the value of time for not having to defend himself in court. Few traffic violators who pull over in response to the ominous flashing light would conclude that they did not obtain something of value if the officer, after hearing the driver's "reason" for the infraction, let the offender go without writing a ticket.

We note that our interpretation of section 912 comports with the statute's general purpose articulated by the Supreme Court. Both types of section 912 offenses described in *Kimberlin* require both a pretense and an act. *See, e.g., United States v. Harmon,* 496 F.2d 20 (2d Cir., 1974) (an indictment charging false impersonation without alleging that the defendant acted in conformity with his pretended character or obtained anything of value held insufficient). The statute does not punish mere puffing. However, "[i]t is the false pretense of Federal authority that is the mischief to be cured...." *Barnow,* 239 U.S. at 78. That mischief is the same whether the impersonator swindles a widow out of $4000 as in *Honea* or dupes a police officer out of issuing a ticket.

Our study of the word "obtain" does not end our analysis. In the second part of his argument, Rippee contends that he is exempt from liability under section 912 because even assuming he did obtain benefits, those benefits accrued to him in his personal capacity and not as a representative of the United States Marshals Service. Rippee maintains that "[a]ssuming, arguendo, that [he] ... obtained any benefits at all, these benefits would accrue to him in his personal capacity. Even if he had been a Marshal, whether he received a traffic ticket or not was certainly of no concern to the federal government or the United States Marshal's [sic] Service." (Appellant's Reply Brief at 3). The Ninth Circuit and the Second Circuit have rejected similar arguments. In *Littell v. United States,* 169 F. 620 (9th Cir., 1909), the defendant obtained board, lodging and a loan of $600 for a personal investment on the basis of his statement that he was in town to oversee construction of the Federal Building and other government works. The Ninth Circuit held that although the benefits the defendant obtained accrued to him personally, the predecessor statute to section 912 reached the defendant's conduct. *Id.* at 622. Relying in part on *Littell,* the Second Circuit rejected a comparable argument in *Etheridge* where the defendant obtained a personal loan from Army Emergency Relief by falsely representing that he was a member of the [armed forces]. Likewise, we find it irrelevant that the benefit that Rippee received was conferred on him as an individual and not as a representative of the United States Marshals Service.

As authority for his contrary position, Rippee cites *United States v. Grewe,* 242 F.Supp. 826 (W.D.Mo., 1965) and *United States v. York,* 202 F.Supp. 275 (E.D.Va., 1962). In *York* and *Grewe,* the defendants pretended to be employed by the United States but did not assert that they were acting under federal authority at the time they obtained a benefit. In *York,* the defendant, a teenage girl, obtained credit to buy a dress by listing her employer as the FBI. The court held that her conduct did not constitute a violation of section 912. While the defendant pretended to be an employee of an agency of the United States, she did not pretend " 'to be an officer or employee *acting under the authority of the United States or any department, agency, or officer thereof* '" because she never represented that she was buying the dress under the authority of the FBI. *York,* 202 F.Supp. at 276 (quoting 18 U.S.C. §912) (emphasis in original). Similarly, in *Grewe,* the defendant cashed checks for personal obligations and personal funds using a counterfeit United States Army identification card. *Grewe,* 242 F.Supp. at 828. The court pointed out that the defendant falsely represented "only that she '*was employed* by the United States.' " *Id.* at 828 (emphasis in original). Noting the "vast factual difference between representing that one is 'acting under the authority of the United States' and merely representing that one is 'employed by the United States,' " the court dismissed the indictment. *Id.* at 829.

Rippee's reliance on *York* and *Grewe* is misplaced. The defendants in *York* and *Grewe* were outside the reach of section 912 not because they benefitted in their personal capacity from their pretense but because they had not pretended to be employees "acting under the authority of the United States." Correctly construed, the reasoning in *York* and *Grewe* could apply if Rippee's indictment alleged that Rippee stated he was on his way to a picnic and mentioned that his employer was the United States Marshals Service in the hopes that this would influence the National City police officer. Rippee's indictment, however, alleged that he "did falsely assume and pretend to be an officer and employee of the United States acting under the authority thereof." As factual support of this allegation, the indictment stated that Rippee "told National City Illinois police officers that he was a Deputy United States Marshal on his way to assist in the breakup of a fight in progress at Fannies' Night Club...." Therefore, the indictment alleged that Rippee violated section 912 by falsely representing not only that he was an employee of the United States but also that he was acting under the authority of his position at the time he was stopped. Whether or not a United States Marshal's responsibilities actually include breaking up fights does not matter. The indictment alleges that Rippee pretended to be breaking up the fight in his capacity as a Marshal. That is enough to state a violation of the statute. Since Rippee appeals the sufficiency of the indictment but not the sufficiency of the evidence at trial, we do not need to address whether the government produced support for its allegations on the record.[1]

III. Conclusion

Since Rippee's indictment alleged that he obtained forbearance from the National City police officers by impersonating an officer acting under the authority of the United States, the indictment sufficiently stated a violation of 18 U.S.C. §912. Accordingly, we AFFIRM the defendant's conviction.

Case Brief Template

Case Title and Location:
Parties:
Procedural History:
Facts:
Issue:
Summary of Arguments:
Holding:
Court's Rationale:
Court's Order:
Thoughts/Comments:

Have you finished your brief? Let's see how it compares to mine. I note, for the record, that I'm not holding myself out as an expert briefer or as someone who has any knowledge of this area of the law. My comments and questions are in square brackets: I normally would not include them in a brief, but I thought you might find it helpful if you could hear some of my internal dialogue with the court as I read the case. Also, you'll see that I used the "delta"

---

1. Furthermore, we note that the record on appeal does not contain a transcript of the trial but only a transcript of the closing arguments. Rippee has limited us to examination of the indictment and precluded our examination of the evidence produced at trial.

symbol (Δ) instead of "defendant." Some people also use pi (π), for "plaintiff." You can use any symbols you want, as long as you remember what they mean when you read your brief later.

Sample Case Brief

Case Title and Location:	United States of America v. Rippee [this is probably a criminal case, because the United States is a party] 961 F.2d 677 (7th Cir., 1992) [*This case must come from the federal courts, because it's published in F.2d, which stands for Federal Reporter, Second Series. It was decided by the Seventh Circuit Court of Appeals, and it's from 1992, which means it's fairly old. I wonder if this is still good law or whether it's been superseded by a more recent case. Whom does this opinion bind? The Seventh Circuit controls federal district courts in Illinois, Indiana, and Wisconsin, and since this is a Court of Appeals decision, it can't bind any of the other circuit courts or the Supreme Court. Because this is a federal case from the Court of Appeals, it won't bind any state courts.*]
Parties:	United States of America is the Plaintiff/Appellee, and Robert Rippee is the Defendant/Appellant. [*That means that Rippee lost on the lower level, because he is the one who invoked the appellate court's jurisdiction. That's confirmed by the procedural history of the case.*]
Procedural History:	Grand jury in the Southern District of Illinois indicted defendant on February 21, 1991. Case went to trial and jury convicted. Judge sentenced defendant to seven months in prison "pursuant to the Sentencing Guidelines." Δ appealed. [*Do all criminal cases need an indictment from a grand jury? Or is that just true of federal criminal cases? What are the sentencing guidelines?*] The decision was written by Judge Manion.
Facts:	Δ was stopped for making illegal turn on January 1, 1991 [*I wonder if enforcement was particularly tight for the New Year holiday*] by police officers from National City. [*So these were local police. I wonder if he'd have tried this with state troopers or, if he had, if they would have believed him*]. Δ claimed to be a United States Marshal on his way to break up a fight and police let him go

without a ticket. [*They must have found out at some point that he wasn't a Marshal, but the case doesn't tell us how this happened. The court notes in the footnote at the end of the opinion that it wasn't given a transcript of the trial and that Δ "limited" the court to an examination of the indictment and "precluded" it from examining the trial evidence. Is it the appellant's responsibility to get the appellate court the transcript of the trial? Could the court not get that directly from the trial court? Is this why the facts are so limited?*]

Issue: Whether avoiding a penalty is the same as obtaining a thing of value, and whether an individual acting for personal benefit, not as a representative of the United States, has violated 18 U.S.C. §912. [*What is 18 U.S.C.? It's Title 18 of the United States Code, which is where most federal criminal statutes are codified.*]

Summary of Arguments: Δ argues that most cases under §912 involve people getting things by deceitful means, and that since he didn't actually get anything, and only avoided something (a traffic ticket) his conduct can't be sanctioned under the statute. Alternatively, Δ argues that even if he got a benefit, it accrued to him in his personal capacity, not as a representative of the Marshal's service.

Holding: Yes. The word "obtain" includes within its meaning the avoidance of a criminal penalty, and falsely claiming to be acting under the authority of the federal government is enough to violate §912.

Court's Rationale: Issue (1): When you persuade the police to not give you a traffic ticket, you obtain something of value because you don't have to face the consequences of that ticket—like a fine, a raise in insurance premiums, or an appearance in court. [*Is that really a "thing of value?" The appellate court and the trial court both seem to emphasize the benefits of not going to court, but that seems to be the weakest of the things of value you might obtain. Do we know for sure that this Δ would have been given a ticket? It was just an illegal U-turn. Maybe the police would have let him off with a warning. If he had paid the ticket, he wouldn't have had to go to court, so does the court's deci-*]

sion make sense here? Is this why the court is saying that it can't look at the sufficiency of the evidence at trial? If Δ is limiting his claim to the sufficiency of the indictment, maybe these details don't matter in this case. I wonder if things would be different if he had claimed the evidence wasn't sufficient either.]

Issue (2): It didn't matter that Δ received a benefit in his personal capacity, not in his alleged official capacity as a Marshal. Although Δ cited to two cases, [*both of them from F. Supp., meaning that they were federal district courts, neither of them from districts in the Seventh Circuit, and both decisions from around thirty years before this case was decided. There can't have been much law to help these arguments*] neither helped Δ because in neither case had the Δ claimed to be acting under authority of the federal government, only that they were employed by the federal government. Δ here said he was going to break up a fight in his capacity as a U.S. Marshal, and that was enough to violate the statute. [*So if he had just had a sign on his visor saying "U.S. Marshal," would that have been a successful defense? Or if he had said, "Can you cut me a break? I'm a U.S. marshal" Would that make this case more like the cases Δ cited?*]

Court's Order: Conviction affirmed. [*Implying the sentence was affirmed as well.*]

Thoughts/Comments: I know you have to stop people from pretending to be federal officers, but does seven months in jail seem a little harsh for a guy trying to get out of a traffic ticket? What if he'd said he was a state trooper? Would the penalty have been the same? The court in the *York* case found that there wasn't a violation of the statute, but I wonder if its thinking was influenced by the fact that the Δ in that case was a teenage girl, so her claim to be in the FBI would not have been very credible. Does the fact that the officers believed the Δ make a difference? If the police officers had asked this Δ for ID at the traffic stop and he hadn't been able to show any, would he have been guilty of a violation under §912? The police probably would have given him the ticket for the illegal U-turn, so would he have obtained anything of value?

Once they found out that he wasn't a Marshal, did they give him a ticket? If they did, did he really get anything of value by his deception? He didn't get the ticket right away, but if he got one in the end, he would still have to pay the fine, go to court, and pay the higher insurance premiums. Can the police really control the outcome of this case by their decision to give him a ticket or not?

Did your brief look like mine? Did you have the same questions or different ones? As with so many things in law school, the work is more important than the result, the journey is more important than the destination. If we have gone through the process of reading this case carefully, we can have an intelligent discussion about the case by asking each other our questions. If we were in class with someone who teaches criminal law, their questions would guide us through the case and help us see its significance in the broader context of whatever part of the law we were studying at the time.

That's why canned briefs are a waste of your money. They give you a brief of the case, to be sure, but that's just a crutch, and it's the least important aspect of case briefing. Creating the brief—the questions you ask and the answers you come up with—is what is important. The person who created a commercial brief got a tremendous benefit from creating these briefs, but you won't get any of that benefit because you didn't do the work yourself. The best technique is to do the work yourself. If you do, you won't need a crutch at all.

Working through the cases yourself helps you understand something else as well, something that's not important for your performance in law school but which—I think—is one of the most important lessons you can learn about the law: Cases are about *people*, not legal abstractions. We use cases like the one reproduced here to learn legal doctrine and explore nuances in the law. It's easy to forget that the court's decision has a profound impact on the litigants or, in a criminal case like Mr. Rippee's, the defendant. Although we emphasize the importance of the facts of a case, because the facts can change the way a court rules, we tend to forget that these things happened to a real person. That disconnection of the case from real life becomes more profound when we're not even reading the case but someone's commercially prepared brief of it. The people involved in the case really don't matter now, it's just what the case can tell us about torts, contracts, or criminal law.

This is an understandable reaction, and a necessary one; if you thought about all the pain and suffering embodied in all the cases you read, you would never get anything done because you would be in a psychologist's office for the duration of law school. It's all right to treat these cases more as laboratory experiments than as being windows into people's lives while you're trying to understand the legal principles involved.

All the same, try not to forget that the cases involved real people and real problems. In Mr. Rippee's case, for example, we read about a man who made a foolish—almost ludicrous—mistake. It's hard to imagine any competent police officer thinking for a second that a U.S. Marshal, of all law enforcement agents, would be on his way to stop a fight at a bar—that's just not what U.S. Marshals do. The risk so far outweighed the potential reward of evading a moving violation ticket that no one would take the chance if they gave the matter a moment's thought. But Rippee undeniably made that mistake, and the decision meant that he paid for his moment of craziness with seven months in prison.

That conviction will haunt him in other ways as well; he won't be able to own or be in close proximity to any kind of firearm, his right to vote was taken away (at least for a time), and he will have to disclose to every potential employer and on pretty much every official form he fills in for the rest of his life that he has a criminal record for impersonating a federal officer. I'm not saying that Mr. Rippee didn't deserve the penalty he received, nor am I saying that the collateral consequences of his actions are improper either, but as we read the Seventh Circuit decision that confirmed his conviction and sentence, it's important to keep in the back of our minds that he suffered those consequences. Remembering that cases affect real people forces us to concentrate on the importance of our role as lawyers to our clients—whether they're individuals, like Mr. Rippee, or the state, like the Assistant United States Attorney who prosecuted the case. It reminds us that our actions have real-world consequences for real people. As you brief cases for law school, try to spare a thought for the people involved and what they must have been feeling as their case made its passage through the judicial system.

Of course, briefing cases like this can take a long time, although you will get faster at briefing with more practice. The time and the effort involved in reading the cases this closely is what drives many students to stop briefing cases. Many of you will stop briefing cases as well, probably fairly soon after you start your first semester. If you resist the temptation to take things a little easier, though. and if you decide to keep working at your case reading and briefing, you will be better off once exams start.

> **Exercise:** Brief one case each day until you start law school. Pick short cases to work on and don't worry about their doctrinal significance. They should be short enough to allow you to practice your briefing skills without eating up your entire day. As you brief a case, try to take the process as seriously as you would if this case was going to be a central

part of a class discussion tomorrow. Read the case carefully and actively, trying to suck out every piece of information contained in the case. Think about what you know about the facts and the law, think about whether there is anything you're not being told, think about how the opinion is written, predict what's going to happen, and then test your prediction against the actual result and the rationale the court gives for reaching its decision.

5

Note Taking

So it's your first day in law school, you've briefed all your cases for the first class—because you know that most law school professors expect you to work right from the beginning of the first class—you're in the classroom, and the professor walks in and starts to speak. What do you do now? "Start taking notes" is the obvious answer, but it's not necessarily as simple as that. For one thing, a really organized law student started taking notes for this class well before it began. There is also the question of what you're going to use to take notes—should you use pen and paper or a laptop that you have to own as a law student? Should you be using a recording device so you can listen to the class again later? Finally, there's the question of what you should be taking notes about. Should you be transcribing every word or only noting what seems important to you?

Taking notes probably wasn't on your list of things to worry about. This is surely the same skill that you've been employing since elementary school, and it stood you in demonstrably good stead; you are coming to law school, for goodness sake! As you will learn quickly, though, the only foolish thought in law school is the unexamined one, and the greatest enemy of a law student is the reflexive assumption. Some professors believe that many students don't take good notes, based on what they see in exams. Even with something as apparently simple and straightforward as taking notes in class, try to improve on what you did before and make your notes more helpful in your quest to get the best grades possible.

A. When to Start Taking Notes

Although many law students start taking notes once the professor says something that sounds noteworthy, I don't believe that's the most efficient practice. Instead, I suggest that you start taking notes *before* the class starts each day. It's a great way to really engage yourself in the material you are going to be covering, and being engaged is the best way to learn something (as opposed to just hearing it).

Case briefing in the methodical way described in Chapter 4 can cause some unintended problems if you're not careful. You will probably brief the cases for, say, a torts class at several different times before the class starts, and you'll probably be finished with your preparation the evening before the class. That's a good idea, because you've given yourself enough time to really think about the cases and work through the thorny issues they present. But it also means that you might have forgotten some details of the earlier cases by the time you get to the later cases, and you might not have identified the thread that connects all the materials for a particular class.

One way to fix that problem is to designate a time as close to class as possible to go over the briefs you have prepared, read the textbook commentary (if there is one) on those cases, and think about how what you're doing in this class ties in with what you learned in your previous classes. If you're going to do that, why not take notes to help you remember your thoughts? If you're going to take notes, let them form the start of your notes for class. That way, when you go back over your notes toward the end of the semester, as you're preparing for exams, you will remember what you thought you had learned previously, what you thought you were going to learn in the class, and—when you look at the start of your notes for the next class—you'll learn how correct you were in your prediction for what you knew and what you were going to learn.

This type of note taking is very helpful in the learning process because it's recursive in nature. You're going back over your previous class and your briefs for the coming class and putting them in the context of what you had already learned. That will help embed the knowledge into your memory. By doing this constantly—reading, taking notes, reflecting on what you've learned, and tying it in to what you're going to learn next—you give yourself the chance to understand not just the fine details of the individual cases but also their place in the broader framework of the subject.

If you do this carefully and thoughtfully for every class, you will find that exam preparation is simple because you'll already know almost everything you need to know, and it's available for quick recall. You'll still have some work to do, of course, but you'll be surprised at how well and how easily you can remember details of what your professor said about a case or a subject. In fact, you'll be surprised at how well you can recall this material years later, when you review it before taking the bar exam. That's when you'll really be happy you made the effort to learn how to learn as efficiently as possible.

Following this practice also helps make the information in your briefs available to you at times of stress, such as when your professor calls on you in class. You have surely had the experience of thinking that you knew something well but then forgetting that information when called on to tell someone about it.

That happened not because you didn't know what you were being asked about—
you probably remembered exactly what you should have said after the moment was over and it was too late—but because you hadn't taken the steps
necessary to make those memories immediately accessible.

The best way to do that is to set your case briefs aside for a while and then
use what you learned in them as the basis for your preliminary notes for the
next class. In this way, you put what you have learned into your own words.
That's one of the best ways to make sure you've really learned something and
that the information is going to be available to you when next you need to recall it, even if you're under stress when you need to drag it up from your memory.

> **Exercise:** Read a news story every day about something that's hap-
> pening in the country or in the world. Make notes about the story,
> much as you would brief a case. Review that brief later, taking notes
> that require you to put the story into your own words. Try to explain
> to someone—a friend, your spouse, or your parents—what the story
> was about, encouraging them to ask questions when they don't un-
> derstand something. There will always be some details about the story
> you won't be able to know, of course, because no story stands alone
> and you would have to follow it for a long time to get all the necessary
> context. If you do follow a story for a while—and there is almost al-
> ways a story running for weeks in the national press—you will find
> yourself becoming quite fluent in the facts and the underlying issues.

B. How to Format Your Notes

If you start taking notes before class begins, you will have to find a way to
show where the preclass notes end and the actual class notes start. In the days
before computers, this was simple; you could make your preclass notes in, say,
red ink and your in-class notes in blue or black ink. You can do that with computers as well, of course, but a simpler solution might be using one font for
the preclass notes and a separate font for the in-class notes. You could also ital-
icize the preclass notes, or use any of the other quick formatting options available to you. As with case briefs, the important thing is that the notes are yours;
anything that helps you remember is good, anything that distracts you or does-
n't help you is bad.

There are, however, some things that should be in all of your notes. Every
page should have, at a minimum, the name of the course (torts, contracts,

and so on) and the date of the particular class that you're taking notes on. Putting the professor's name on your notes is probably a good idea as well, not because you'll forget his or her name but because doing this will become a good habit. In the future, when you take notes of a meeting with a partner at a law firm or during a client meeting or a court hearing, you will automatically make a note of the person whose meeting or hearing it was. Those names might not be familiar to you, and sometimes you might forget that important detail.

If you are using a computer to take notes, and if your professor's syllabus is available electronically, you might want to cut and paste the relevant entry for the day's class at the start of your notes. This will remind you of what pages from the textbook the class session covered, as well as any other information your professor might have included. Even if you can't cut and paste in this information, it's helpful to note what textbook pages were covered in your notes; this can save you flipping through your book, looking for cases and commentary when you want to revise the material at the end of the semester.

If you're taking notes on paper, you might also consider putting "page __ of __" at the top of the page. When class is over, count how many total pages of notes you have, and then go back and fill in the blanks: "page 1 of 3, page 2 of 3, page 3 of 3," for example. If you're using a computer, you can set up a header to record this information so that when you print out your notes, the page information will be inserted automatically. Pages can get lost in the process of transferring them from notepad to notebook, and sometimes notes can be so fragmentary that it can be difficult to tell whether information has been lost. Knowing how many pages are supposed to be there can help you decide if a page or two is missing or if you just took notes that are difficult to understand. For the same reason, you might consider putting your name on each page of your notes as well. You might not want someone to know whose notes they have found, but that's better than losing your notes and not being able to re-create them later.

You should also number your class notes globally, meaning that at the end of the semester, each page of your class notes is numbered consecutively, with page 1 being the first page of your notes on the first day of classes and page x being the last page of the whole semester of class notes. This will enable you to cross-reference your notes in your outlines.

It's good to have two separate areas for note taking on each page. You can do this on a computer, especially with a specialized note taking program, but it's easier on paper. Some notepads come with extra-wide margins—dividing the page into a left side of approximately one-third and a right side of approximately two-thirds of the page. These pads are hard to find even in large office supply stores, but you can find them sometimes in smaller stores or places that cater particularly to lawyers. Lawyers sometimes create their own divided notepads by simply drawing a line down the middle of a page.

Having a page divided like this allows you to take two different types of notes. On the larger, right-hand side of the page you can take notes from class as you would regularly, while on the smaller, left-hand side of the page you can record your thoughts and comments about the class. This doesn't mean you should write down "I'm bored" or "It's too hot/cold/light/dark/something in here." If your professor says something you don't understand, or if you can predict where the professor is going with a line of questioning, you can record that thought and see if you can clarify your confusion, or if you were correct in your prediction, after class is over.

C. Computer, Paper, and Recording

I have mentioned some potential differences between taking notes on computer and on paper, and here I address the issue head-on. Is it better for you to take notes using one format or the other? What are the pros and cons of each approach? Does it make sense to record classes so you can listen to them again later? As you will see, this is an area with few easy answers.

1. Recording

The question about recording might be the most straightforward to answer. Put simply, whatever the pluses and minuses of recording might be, many of your professors will not allow you to do it. They probably have some language in their syllabus about their decision, and many will say that you may not record their class in any form—audio or video—without their express permission. There are reasons for this, but they are a moot point; once professors have made a decision like this, you're probably not going to be able to talk them out of it by challenging their rationale. If you have a specific reason for wanting to record class—a condition that makes it difficult to take notes, for example—you should explain those special circumstances to your professor or to the office in your law school that deals with issues like this. Sometimes students know that they will miss class ahead of time and ask permission for another student to record the class for them, and sometimes professors will grant permission for that reason. If you don't get permission, and your professor has said you may not record class, then recording is not an option for you.

Even if your professor allows you to record classes, you still might not want to. If you take good notes and are careful to do good preparation for each class, it shouldn't be necessary for you to listen to an entire class again to be sure you understood everything. If you missed something, you can ask your professor if it's possible for him or her to address your area of confusion. Other students might be able to help you work through something you didn't understand, although be careful about this—sometimes they are as confused as you, but they don't know it. Under almost all circumstances, it's better to know that you don't understand something than to not know you don't understand something. You might want to be cautious about enlisting your classmates to explain something to you, unless you are certain that they know something you don't.

2. Computers and Pens

Before we start on this strangely emotional subject, let me confess something. I'm a Baby Boomer, born in the 1950s, and I went through every phase of my education—from kindergarten to law school—without once seeing a computer in a classroom. Every note I ever took as a school student, undergraduate, graduate, or law student was handwritten. I remember the first TV commercials for IBM's personal computer, and the first computer I owned was a nonportable 128k Macintosh.

By contrast, you are most likely one of the millennial generation, and you have been familiar with computers during every phase of your education. Your cell phone has orders of magnitude more processing power than did my original Mac. You probably feel comfortable with all forms of communication devices.

You will notice that I didn't suggest that every note you took in school and college was taken on a computer, because experience tells me that isn't the case. Most law students I meet took handwritten notes prior to law school and that affects the advice I offer to you now: Consider taking notes in law school the same way you took notes as undergraduates. If that means that you took notes using pen and paper, then consider continuing to do this as law students.

As with recording classes, this decision might be made for you by your professor. There's been a substantial backlash against laptops in the classroom recently, and many professors are banning them. They have good reasons for doing so; some preliminary studies suggest that students who take notes using pen and paper during class do better on law school exams than do students who use computers. And professors report that the quality of class discussion is much improved when no student in the class is using a computer. Whether you agree with the results of these studies or not, if your professor bans laptops in the classroom, there's probably not much you can do about it.

Personally, I'm not a Luddite. I think computers are very useful machines, so much so that I'm writing this book on my desktop computer at home. Nor is my suggestion that you use what you're familiar with to take notes driven by a concern that too many students use their computers for, let's say, non-class-related activities during class. It's true that too many students do this, and they're behaving foolishly and discourteously when they do; law school is too difficult, and costs too much money, for you to spend your time in class surfing the Internet, checking email, and texting friends. As one who stands in front of students each semester, let me assure you that we know when you're doing these things. And your fellow students know it as well; you're distracting them with your web surfing or emailing, and that really isn't fair to them.

Of course, if you want to waste your time and money by not paying attention in class, you'll find ways to do that even if you don't have a computer with you. I knew people in law school who would get through the *New York Times* and *Washington Post* crosswords during classes and others who would bring books and magazines to read behind their textbooks. They didn't do well in law school, but I suppose they were entertained.

I suggest that you take notes in class the same way you've always done for a simple reason: Whatever you did worked for you, and law school is too difficult, the material too unfamiliar, and the press of work too great right from the beginning for you to try to master a new way of learning. Why make your lives more difficult than they already are? Better to focus on improving the note taking skills you already possess than to try to learn completely new ones. So if you have used computers in the classroom before, and you're certain that you can take good notes using them, you should be perfectly comfortable using them to take notes in law school as well. But if you're familiar with pen and paper in the classroom, by all means, continue to use them. You might think you look old-fashioned compared to the student with the new laptop sitting next to you. But you'll probably be taking better notes, and besides, unless you brought a crossword with you, you're probably going to be less tempted to let your attention wander.

Taking notes with pen and paper doesn't mean that your notes need to stay in that form, of course. One of the most important things you can do with your notes is to go back over them once you've taken them, and transcribing your written notes to computer is the perfect time to do that. Before you can review and transcribe your notes, though, you have to take them. We'll talk about that next.

Exercise: If you want to see what note taking with a computer will be like, find out *before* law school rather than during it. Watch a news broadcast on television for a week, taking notes on a computer on every story on every broadcast. Ideally, the program should be at least an hour long and have no commercial breaks; the goal is to simulate the duration and continuous nature of a law school class as closely as possible. The day after you take your notes, but before the next broadcast, go over your notes and see how much you can recall. Can you remember the details of each story, or do you have just a general sense of what each story was about? As you evaluate your note-taking performance, remember that the most complex news report on television is substantially easier to understand than a normal law school class.

Once you have done this for a week, switch note-taking styles and take notes by hand for another week. Compare your level of understanding to the previous week. Is it the same? Do you feel you have learned more or less effectively using one note-taking method or the other? Which method was easier for you? What you learn during this exercise might be helpful in deciding what note-taking medium to use in law school.

D. The Content of Your Notes

However you take notes, you have to decide what to include and what to leave out. This is a personal decision, and a very important one—your notes might be meaningless if you leave out a crucial piece of information, yet they will be equally meaningless if you take down too much information, leaving yourself with an undifferentiated clump of data with no idea of what is and isn't important.

Let's figure out where the boundaries for effective note taking might lie. We can guess that you don't want to reduce the entire class to one word, because no single word could encapsulate the complexity of even the limited amount of legal doctrine you cover in a single class. Similarly, we can agree that you do not want to transcribe every word said in every class, because you won't have the time to read and analyze your notes afterward and you'll be stuck with an impossible task when it comes time to synthesize your notes to prepare for exams.

Working inward from these extremes, we can see that the ideal set of notes for a class records enough information to remind you of each important point that was discussed without including any extraneous discussion. You should also record your own questions about the class discussion and what your professor is saying, even if those questions are answered later in the class (this is what the left side of your paper is for—to record your thoughts and commentary on the class discussion, which you're recording on the larger, right-hand side of the paper).

You shouldn't be in any doubt that your professor's voice is the most important one in the class. Not only does he or she know more about the topic than anyone else in the room, the professor also sets the final exam. Even if you disagree with his or her perspective on a particular issue (and that can happen, although if it does, you should examine your own opinions very carefully to see if your logic holds up under scrutiny), be sure to note what your professor says about the issue because *that's* the opinion that will earn you a good grade.

This doesn't mean you should record every word your professor says, but it does mean you should record the salient aspects of the discussion. As you do that, also ask yourself the same types of questions you would be asking if you were reading a transcript of the class. On the left side of the page, record your impressions of the direction the discussion is taking, whether you agree with something a classmate says when called on, what you understand and—more important—what you *don't* understand about a particular issue, and what you predict will be the final outcome of the discussion.

You should be darting between the left and right sides of the page regularly, using the time when there isn't something of note to record to go write down your thoughts and impressions on the left side of the page. Sometimes that might mean waiting several minutes for a lull in the class discussion before you can go back and take down some thoughts about something that happened earlier. You have to do this *during* class. Unless you have a perfect memory, you'll forget the comment you wanted to make if you wait until later to record it.

You will work hard in class, hopping back and forth between your case briefs, your textbook, and your class notes, paying close attention to what's being said, thinking about what you have just heard, predicting what you are about to hear, and recording both the salient aspects of the class discussion and your own thoughts, questions, and comments. Being an active participant in a law school class is hard work, even if you don't say a word. If you take notes in this way, you might be tired at the end of class; this is a demanding process and until you get used to it, you can feel drained at the end of class and exhausted by the end of the day. Don't worry—you will get in shape pretty quickly, and this will become easier over time. If you take notes in this way, of course, there won't be any time to goof around and lose focus.

A quick note on organizing your class notes. Your notes should be coordinated, as closely as possible, with your textbook and case briefs. If you're going to discuss, for example, the *Palsgraf* case halfway through your torts class on a particular day, and you have briefed the version of *Palsgraf* contained in your textbook, your notes should have a distinct visual break when you stop talking about the previous case and start talking about *Palsgraf,* and you should write the case name (and, ideally, the page number of the textbook where the case begins) in your notes before you start to record the discussion. That way, you can easily find the case, your brief, and your class notes when you're studying for exams.

E. Note Review

Class is over, and you've recovered somewhat from the mental gymnastics you were performing as you took notes. Unfortunately, the end of class doesn't mean the end of the note-taking process. Just as you should begin taking notes before class starts, you should stop taking notes well after class is done. The recursive learning model I've been emphasizing throughout this book demands that you go back over the material you covered in class to embed it in your memory.

The best time to do this is at least a couple of hours after class is over and well before your next class on this subject—ideally right before you start reading and briefing the material for your next class in that course. You should reread your notes, think about the questions you had, and see if you can answer those questions now or if you are still unsure. If you can't answer your own questions, do you think the next class will give you the information to answer them, or is your confusion more fundamental than that? Think about the notes you have taken on the right side of your pages; do you recall the professor saying those things? Can you recall in your mind how the class discussion went during the time you were taking these notes? If you can remember the discussion after the trigger of reading your class notes, it's likely that you'll remember the discussion in a month or so, once you start preparing the material for upcoming exams. Good note taking, you will discover, allows you to re-create the important points of a class discussion months after it took place; this skill is much more valuable that just recording the class and listening passively to what happened.

If you took your notes by hand, this is a good time to type them up and save them in your computer. Rewriting your notes is one of the best ways of re-engaging with the material and helping it stick in your memory. Editing your notes is an even better practice than simply retyping them, expanding them if necessary (I recommend using a different font, if possible, to remind you of the difference between notes taken in class and revisions of notes made after class was over) and answering questions you had while class was going on.

This re-engagement with your class notes is the perfect prelude to preparing your case briefs for the next class. Once you have completed your involvement with your notes, you will remember exactly what happened previously, so now you can test what you're reading for the next class with what you already know about the law. One of the most important aspects of case briefing is the practice of slotting what you are reading into the framework of what you have learned before, and the best way to do that is to reread your notes immediately before you begin briefing the materials for your next class.

6

Outlining

The outlining process is something you cannot begin until you have studied for several weeks. My intent was to write something here that would help you spend some time in the summer preparing for law school, not something about how to survive once you started law school. But the more I wrote about case briefing and note taking, the more I realized it would be helpful if we talked about outlines—the documents that are the culmination of your class preparation and in-class notating you'll be doing. It's easier to understand the journey if you know something about the destination.

This chapter is a short and cursory look at class outlines, the exam preparation instrument of choice among law students. It comes with the usual caution that any such document is, by its nature, intensely personal. From your perspective, the best outline ever prepared hasn't been written yet, because it's the one you will write to help you do well in your exams. Other outlines might be better organized, neater, or more informative, but that doesn't matter at all to you; all that's important is that your outline is organized appropriately *for you* and contains the material *you need* to do well. As with your case briefs and class notes, no one will grade your outline.

The personal nature of outlines, like case briefs and class notes, is the reason you need to prepare them yourself. There are commercial outlines available, and your classmates (and upper-class students) will probably have course outlines that might be available to you, sometimes free, and sometimes for a fee. But reading someone else's outline, no matter how well organized and detailed it might be, is a poor substitute for preparing your own outline. As with many other things in law school, the work you do in preparing the outline is much more important than the eventual result, because that's what helps you grapple with the material and (one hopes) understand it better. An outline can help you remember some of the details that you might forget under the pressure of exam preparation, but the fundamental elements of the course can only be wired into your brain as the result of your hard work during the outlining process.

With that introduction, let's talk about outlines. Some books about the law school experience seem to spend an inordinate amount of time talking about outlines and reading them, and it's easy to imagine that students spend all their time and energy worrying about creating the perfect outline. Relax! there's no magic to outlining, and if you have done a good job with your case briefs and class notes, outlining a course will be a relatively simple and very helpful task for you.

A. When to Start Outlining

It's important that you *not* start outlining too early in the semester. Some students start outlining in their first week of classes, but that usually doesn't do them much good because what they learn in the second week causes them (or should cause them) to go back and rework their outline for the first week. This happens each week.

The best time to start outlining is once you reach a logical transition in the coursework. There aren't many first-year courses that are seamless, moving from one week to the next without any divisions in material. In torts, for example, you will probably cover negligence, strict liability, and several other broad areas within the subject. These areas will likely be designated as such in your syllabus, and you'll know from your textbooks as well when you move from one area to another.

As with most things in life, transitions in law school offer a chance for retrospection and reflection. That's the perfect time to start outlining, because outlines are all about retrospection and reflection. It's possible that the first few classes in a new area of torts or contracts might teach you something about the previous area, but it's also possible they will be quite separate as well. Because it's less likely that next week's classes will change what you thought you knew about the previous week's classes, this is a good time to go back over the previous weeks of material and try to draw together the details and the common threads that ran through your classes on that subject.

"Drawing together" is actually the perfect description of the outlining process, because what you are doing is going back over an area in a course—torts, say—and trying to get an overview of the entire area, trying to separate the forest from the trees. While you were studying the material, it was difficult to step back and see the whole picture, just as it's difficult for a weaver to see the entire tapestry when working a single thread into the material. Sometimes the weaver has to stand back and see how that single thread fits into the overall design, and that's what the outlining process is like. The best time to do this is once you have completed one subject area and can get some perspective on what you've discussed. Start too early and you won't know enough about what's coming to make any really intelligent decisions about what you've learned so far; start too late and you'll have forgotten some of the details that would help clarify your understanding of the area.

B. What Form Should Your Outline Take?

It is difficult to say what should be in your outline or how you should organize the material, because every person is different and your outline should be geared to what helps you best. I talk here in general terms about different outlining approaches. If one of these helps suggest an approach that might work for you, that's great, and if you chose to outline in a completely different way, that's fine as well.

The two most widespread styles of outline are the common outline form — what I'll call here the skeleton outline, with headings, subheadings, sub-sub-headings, and so on, written in short sentence fragments — and the narrative outline, which is written in complete sentences and paragraphs and looks more like a miniature treatise on a subject.

1. Skeleton Outlines

The skeleton outline has some significant advantages to it. The most obvious is that the information is readily available to you; you can flip through the various levels of headings quickly and find the information you are looking for with little difficulty. This is especially helpful in open-book exams, where your professor might let you take your outline into the exam room. It is also the type of outline many of you are already familiar with from high school and college. It is good at showing multipart tests and rules, of which there are many in law. If you have learned that a particular tort has five elements, for example, the skeleton outline is the perfect form to record the following.

A. Tort X has the following elements:
    1. _____
    2. _____
    3. _____
    4. _____
    5. _____

As you work through the material, a picture of the bones of the subject (hence "skeleton outline") quickly emerges.

In addition to its advantages, this type of outline has some drawbacks as well. The most obvious of these is related to the very ordering of information that is one of its greatest strengths. Not all legal information divides neatly into multipart tests, and skeleton outlines aren't as helpful in describing such information because they tend to force concepts into boxes, even if the concepts don't fit so well.

Another drawback of the skeleton outline is its terseness, which limits the ability to rehearse the things we would like to say about a topic. Terse language is necessary for a skeleton outline, because too much text would cause it to become too bulky and long. But sometimes we need to write in complete sentences about something to fully understand the material and practice what we'll say about it when asked on an exam. What's a weakness for the skeleton outline, though, is one of the greatest strengths of the narrative outline.

2. Narrative Outlines

The narrative outline is just what it sounds like—a written document that summarizes the content of a subject. In essence, to prepare a narrative outline for a course or part of a course, you take your class notes and case briefs and summarize their content. Although narrative outlines condense the information you have learned about an area, they are still much longer than skeleton outlines. Even when they're organized with headings and subheadings, finding information in them can be more difficult than finding information in skeleton outlines. Because they are written in complete sentences, and therefore take longer to prepare, they can often be more reliable methods of getting information into your long-term memory.

Some students make the mistake of thinking that narrative outlines should be organized chronologically, the outline for class one followed by the outline for class two, class three, and so on. That wouldn't be an outline of a course, or an area of the law, it would just be an outline of your class notes. It is better to take your notes for the entire area of the law and identify the themes that run through all the classes and outline according to those themes, adding in a synthesis of the various cases that illustrate and articulate the concepts in this area, as well as a cross-reference to the notes pages on which the outlined information appears. Once you can organize this information thematically, you will feel confident that you have a good sense of the material and that you'll be able to reproduce what you know about it to others when asked.

The ability to reproduce the concepts you've written about in your narrative is this form of outline's greatest strength. Just as your case briefs help you rehearse what you will say in class about a case if you're asked about it, the narrative outline lets you rehearse what you'll write about if the subject comes up on your exam. If you have done the outlining job correctly, phrases—even complete sentences—will come easily to mind when you create your exam answers. Because they were originally written under less stressful conditions than you face during an exam, they might even be more articulate and more detailed than what you would come up with on your own, in the heat of exam pressure.

3. *The Benefits of Employing Both Outlining Approaches*

Is there a way to get the benefits of both outlining schemes while avoiding the disadvantages of both? There is, although you might not like it. While "belts-and-suspenders" approaches are often frowned on as being unnecessarily duplicative, exam preparation is one area where the word *unnecessarily* doesn't really have a place: the best way to get the benefits of both approaches is to use them both.

This isn't as painful as it might sound, especially if you've been working throughout the semester in a disciplined and organized manner. Again, the approach you follow is entirely up to you; for me, the logical way to do this is to write a narrative outline each time your course hits a logical transition; once the semester is over, go back and prepare a skeleton outline of the narrative outline you have been working on.

This approach has two benefits. First, it forces you to go back over the material and work with it again. You are not simply letting your eyes pass over words you've already written, which can tempt you into reading passively; instead, you force yourself to actively reengage with the material to create something new, and that engagement helps embed information into your memory. Although much of what you're working on at this stage in the semester should be familiar to you already, confirming what you already know should give you a greater sense of confidence.

Second, creating a skeleton outline of your narrative outline gives you a table of contents and an index for the lengthier outline, allowing you to use the skeleton as a quick reference guide to the topic (essentially, an outline of your outline), the narrative outline as a more detailed resource, and your class notes, case briefs (all of which have been cross-referenced by case name or page number in your narrative outline), and textbook as the most detailed information sources. As long as you have been concentrating while you work on these outlines, you should know everything you need to know about the subject by the time your exams come around.

The downside, of course, is that this is a lot of work. On top of all this outlining, you have classes to prepare for, legal research and writing assignments to complete, and a life to try to lead. There is no question that your days will be full. You can't come to law school assuming that you won't have to work hard; that would be unrealistic and foolish, and my experience of law students is that they are neither of these things. What might take you aback is the volume of work expected of you. It really is manageable, though, if you plan for it and commit to doing it. And that's what we'll talk about next.

7

Time Management

Time is something you never have enough of in law school, so time management is one of the most important things you can learn before you come here. For some of you, this might not be a problem. Anyone who has produced work under the pressure of inflexible deadlines knows what the next three years—and, in fact, the rest of their careers as lawyers—will be like. Unless you've experienced constant deadline stress, law school might be an unpleasant surprise for you. Don't worry though: there are plenty of tools to help you prepare in advance and keep the stress to a minimum.

A. Why Time Is at a Premium in Law School

If you've only taken a quick glance at your schedule for the first semester, you might not be expecting there to be much of a time management problem. You will probably be taking four courses—maybe civil procedure, contracts, torts, and legal research and writing, although some law schools have a different set of first-semester courses—and you might be thinking that they can't take up too much time. However, you would be forgetting three things: first, the number of credit hours for those classes means that you will be physically in class a lot; second, you have to fully prepare for each class you attend; and third, your legal research and writing course requires a lot of writing, which has to be done outside of class.

Once you add up the number of hours you'll be in class, preparing for class, and doing your legal research and writing work, and then add in some time to eat and sleep, you might realize that there aren't many free hours left in the week. You have to leave some time free for relaxation and exercise and, if you have a spouse, partner, or a family, you will need to spend time with them as well. All of these things are important; you can't short-change one to give yourself more time for the others. If you do, either your work or your life (and often both) will suffer. We talk later about how you can calculate how much time these essential activities will take each day.

This might sound bleak and depressing, but it shouldn't be. It's true that the work you do is demanding and time-consuming, but, to sound a familiar theme, you knew that law school wouldn't be easy when you sent in your application. Countless others have been through law school and have thrived there. If you come to school prepared and with the right attitude, you will be fine as well.

B. Treat Law School Like a Job

The simplest and most effective way to cope with the pressures of law school is to treat the entire experience as you would a job. This might sound artificial and strange to you, but bear with me as I explain; most practicing lawyers would agree that there are more similarities between law school and work than there are between your previous academic experience and law school.

Treating law school like a job means that you have to be professional about every aspect of your work. At a minimum, this means that you need to be as well prepared as possible for every class, you need to be in class and ready to begin at the scheduled start of class (which means you can't be walking into a 2 pm class *at* 2 pm; that's the time the class begins, and that means you need to be in your seat with your books, notes, and note-taking materials all ready to be used), and you need to submit all work by its due date and time. It shouldn't matter to you if others don't adhere to these standards; all you can do is focus on your own performance. If people in your section come to class late or unprepared, don't be tempted to follow in their footsteps. Let them perform poorly, and be happy you're not making the same mistake.

One crucial step you can take is to identify tasks that must be accomplished and vow to accomplish them in a timely manner. Lawyers know, for example, that they need to reply to client communications—emails, letters, and voicemail messages—as quickly as possible, ideally on the same day they were received. You cannot leave a client hanging, waiting for an answer, no matter how disruptive it might be to your plans for the day. Similarly, if you are a junior associate and a senior partner asks you to do something—research a legal issue, write a memo, sit in on a conference call, and so on—you need to treat that senior lawyer as your client and do whatever you can to accomplish the requested task within the requested timeframe.

You should adopt a similar approach in your dealings with law school faculty, administration, and colleagues. If you have committed to sitting at a table during lunchtime to promote the activities of an association you've joined, for example, you need to honor that commitment, no matter how inconvenient it might be to you. You might think, by the way, that one way to mitigate the effects of such activities is to not join any associations or volunteer to do anything, but I don't recommend you take this drastic step. Although you shouldn't join *every* available organization as soon as you come to law school, there are many student groups and you'll probably find at least one of your interests represented. Joining that organization can put you in touch with students who share your interests or beliefs and who can form the nucleus of a social group for you. If you've joined the organization, then volunteering occasionally to help it meet its goals won't be harmful to you. Like all things, you shouldn't let your volunteer activities dominate your time to the exclusion of your schoolwork, but sensible participation in student activities can be personally and professionally rewarding.

Similarly, if you have made an appointment with a faculty member or a member of the administration, you should keep that appointment at the scheduled time—not too late, and not too early. It might seem unnecessary to give advice like this, but my experience suggests otherwise. The habit of meeting your commitments and responding to communications in a punctual manner will stand you in good stead in your academic and professional life, and it's a relatively painless lesson to learn.

Practicing lawyers know that they don't have a 9–5 job and that they have to work longer hours—sometimes much longer—to get the job done. You should adopt that approach now, because law school makes similar demands on your time. This means that you might not be able to watch as much television as you would like, read as many books, play as many games, or go out as often as you used to. You will still be able to do these things—in fact, you *should* do them because they are the activities that bring you pleasure and relax you, and you'll do much better in school if you're as relaxed and happy as possible. But you won't be able to do them as much, or as often, as you likely are used to.

> **Exercise:** Starting now, try to answer all emails, voicemails, and other communications you receive on the same day you receive them. Even though these might not be business communications, set aside a block of time each day (between 4 and 5 pm, for example) so you can reply to all communications you received during the day before the commonly accepted close of the business day.

C. Plan What Work You're Going to Do and When You'll Do It

Although you should treat law school like a job, there's a crucial difference between the academic and practice worlds: law school is predictable. At the start of each semester, you'll be given syllabi for your classes that will set out, class by class and week by week, the reading you are expected to cover and when written assignments are due. That means you can plan for the work you're going to day by day and week by week.

By contrast, law practice can be frustratingly improvisational. You might have a clear idea of what you want to accomplish on a particular day—write some letters, do research for a memo that's due next week, and write a brief for filing in a couple of days, for example. Your plan might be to get the letters and research out of the way in the morning, leaving yourself the rest of the day for the brief. A calm but still busy day.

Suppose there's a voicemail from a partner waiting for you when you get in, telling you that one of your firm's most important clients has discovered an infringement of a trademark occurring in your part of the country and wants it stopped immediately. Your partner tells you to meet her at 10 am for a conference call with the client, at which you will outline your plan for obtaining an emergency injunction that afternoon. You have no idea what the process for obtaining any form of injunction might be (in fact, you can only vaguely remember injunctions from your first-year civil procedure class), and it's already 9:15, so you only have 45 minutes to research everything and sound intelligent on the conference call. You know that getting everything ready to file for the injunction is going to take not only all of your day but probably the day of several other people at the firm as well.

Obviously, your plan for the day is shot, and you haven't even sat down at your desk yet. In practice, this is a normal state of affairs. I'm not sure if even one day during my time as a practicing lawyer went exactly as I had planned it; there were always phone calls and emails to answer, the mail often brought surprises, and clients and colleagues had questions and things they needed me to do throughout the day. Sometimes the interruptions you experience may be minor, but more often they will involve significant disruptions. Remember, in the example above, you still have some letters to write, a brief coming up in one day sooner than you had before, and research to do. The work you had to do won't go away, and no one else will do it for you. You might be able to do these things tomorrow, assuming that you didn't already have something planned for then, but tomorrow will also bring its own share of surprises and work you weren't expecting.

This doesn't mean you should stop planning, though. In fact, planning is one of the few things that will get you through the hectic life you'll lead as a practicing lawyer, even if you aren't able to execute the plan the way you anticipated. Planning what you're going to do in a day or a week forces you to organize and prioritize all the tasks you have to accomplish, and it gives you a framework for the day around which it might be possible to drape some of the other assignments that come your way. If something comes up that's so disruptive it completely changes your day, you'll know (because you'll have thought about it) how crucial it is that the tasks you had planned for today are and how long they can be delayed.

Mercifully, all of that is for later. Law school, by comparison, has comparatively few surprises, letting you plan out your days, weeks, and even months. You should take advantage of this luxury and plan your work as carefully as possible. This will be very difficult in the first days and weeks of law school; it's almost impossible for you to know, for instance, how long it will take you to do the reading and case briefing for each class until you have some experience under your belt. That is something you'll soon learn, and a plan will help you even in those first few weeks of law school; if nothing else, it will tell you how much work you have to do before you can stop for the evening.

> **Exercise:** Make a plan for the rest of your summer, identifying week-by-week tasks, such as book and equipment buying, arrangements for a move if you're relocating, and the other preparatory steps to accomplish before coming to law school. Review your plan each week to see how closely you were able to stick to your goals and what tasks you were and weren't able to accomplish. Revise your summer plan based on each week's review, and if a task remains undone for more than two weeks, try to identify why you haven't been able to accomplish that task.

D. Maintain an Accurate Calendar

The calendar is a crucial element of a work plan, because it's the only infallible guide to what work has to be done when, and it can show you what's coming up so you can identify any bottlenecks and try to resolve them before they become a problem. Your calendar will become an invaluable lifeline, preventing you from missing deadlines and helping you anticipate when you need to plan for more study time.

Many of you are familiar with calendaring and are comfortable with the idea of recording everything you have to do and when. If you're one of those people, congratulations! For those of you who have survived this long by holding everything in your memory, perhaps referring to a syllabus to help you remember what reading has to be done for tomorrow, it's time to make a change. That approach might have worked up until now, but it will let you down if you rely on it in law school. Because it is impossible to survive as a practicing lawyer without an efficient calendar and planner system, you might as well learn how to calendar events now and become comfortable with a practice that will be with you the rest of your professional career.

There's no magic to keeping an effective calendar. First, you have to have a calendar, and second, you have to record in it every significant event that's coming up in your life. That's it. Whereas it used to be difficult to carry around a calendar big enough to record everything, meaning you had to have at least two calendars—the big one at home and one with you for day-to-day reference—computers have made this much more convenient. You don't need to buy multiple calendars if you use a software package with calendaring capability, and though you might still keep your calendar in two separate locations—on a computer and a cell phone or some other form of PDA, for example—the ability to coordinate the entries electronically means there's little danger of having an entry in one calendar but not the other, something that bedeviled users of paper calendars. Electronic calendars can also store more information than their paper counterparts and can present that information in a variety of different ways. The advent of Internet-based services that allow you to update your calendar by using text messages and phone calls means that you're almost always able to calendar important events as soon as you learn of them.

Keeping your calendar current takes some practice, of course, but you should quickly become comfortable with entering in the date and time of every important event in your personal and professional life. It's crucial to enter the personal dates as well, because it can be easy to forget them given the press of work, and you don't want to forget your spouse's birthday just because you have an legal research and writing assignment due that day. If you're invited to a wedding during the run-up to finals, for example, you will need to know if you can reorganize your work schedule to give yourself the time to attend or if you're going to have to decline the invitation.

Calendars have another useful function for practicing lawyers, especially those who work for firms that bill their clients for the time spent working on a case. Unless you get into the practice of recording the time you spend on an assignment as you go through the day (and I strongly encourage you to get into that practice), it will be very difficult for you to remember, minute by minute, what you did and how long it took you. Even though your day didn't proceed as planned, your calendar can still help as a first step to re-creating a day, and this process can be helpful for you as a law student as well.

You are not billing anyone for your time as a law student, of course, but in addition to being fee-justifying documents, timesheets can serve as useful guides to efficiency. Looking at them, for example, a partner can see when an associate took too long to write a simple letter or—perhaps more important—didn't take enough time. It might seem odd to say that a simple letter didn't take enough time to write, but often the attorney who rushes through seemingly simple tasks hasn't taken the time necessary to proofread a document carefully for mistakes and therefore risks the possibility of a document leaving the office that is unclear or unprofessional. As you'll learn, billing partners can always cut your time if they feel you're taking too long to do something, but most would rather that you record your time accurately and take too long to accomplish a task than have you rush through something (for which they can't add time, for obvious ethical reasons) with the possibility of generating a less-than-perfect work product.

You can learn the same lessons if you record how much time it took you, for example, to read and brief the cases for your torts class tomorrow. If you take a certain amount of time to accomplish that task one week and a substantially less amount of time the next week, you might have become more efficient in your work or you might have been cutting some corners. If you are honest with yourself, you'll know which it is, and if you haven't been taking as much time as you should, you can make an adjustment.

So keep track of your time as you do your work. This practice will allow you to spot trends in your work habits, and soon you'll be able to tell when you're working as efficiently as possible and when you're slipping a little. You might be able to tell this just from the way you feel about your class preparation, but it's always good to have numbers to back up your feelings. Time records are something you will have to get used to eventually; it makes sense to get some practice in keeping them when they are not an essential part of your day. If nothing else, knowing how hard you're working can be helpful if someone—partner, family member, or friend—asks you why you're not as much fun as you used to be.

> **Exercise:** Identify important dates in your life (birthdays, anniversaries, and so on) and enter them into the calendaring system on your computer. Add the dates you know will be important to you over the summer and during school. Any time you have an appointment to keep, make it a habit to enter the date and time into your calendar as soon as possible. Explore some of the options that allow you to make

calendar entries even when you're not at your computer and to get calendar reminders sent to a remote device like your cell phone or email address. Familiarize yourself with all the features of your computer's calendar.

E. Perform a Time Audit

One way to practice recording your time is to perform a time audit. The summer is the perfect time to do this because it can give you some baseline information that you can use to great advantage once you're in law school.

The idea of a time audit is derived from the financial audits experts encourage us to perform to better understand our financial condition, and the mechanics of performing a time audit are as simple as the financial one. For every activity you do during the day, write down the amount of time it took. This doesn't mean you'll be writing in a notebook every second of the day; if you have soup and a salad for dinner, for example, you don't need to record how much time it took you to eat the soup and how much time to eat the salad, just write down the total amount of time it took you to eat dinner. If you watch television while you eat, don't double bill for both activities—double billing is something no lawyer should be accused of. Just write down the time it took to accomplish the principal task—eating dinner, probably, in this example. If you continued to watch television for another hour after dinner, note that time separately so that all the time in your day is recorded.

If you keep careful records for a typical week, you should have all the information you need. Take the amount of sleep for each day and then average that to give you a sense of how much sleep you need each night to be well rested and active the next day. Do the same for essential life activities—eating, for example—and you should end up with an idea of how much time each day you need to live your life. If you subtract that number from 24, you can figure out how much time you have left for everything else.

One of the valuable by-products about this type of audit, of course, is that you're forced to consider what is an "essential life activity" for you. We can all agree that eating is essential, and there some other activities too obvious to mention, but how about exercise, reading a book, or interacting with a child or spouse? Looking carefully at how you spend a week, and then trying to decide whether an activity you perform every day is essential can help you develop a better sense of what is truly important to you. These are activities you can't afford to discontinue when you come to law school without making some fundamental changes in who you are, and that can be vital knowledge.

If you perform this time audit carefully, you'll come to law school armed with much more self-awareness about who you are and how much time it takes to stay that person, and you will know how much time you have to devote to everything else. You can quickly add to that number how much time it takes you to get to and from school every day, and how much time you'll spend in class—absolutes that won't change on a daily basis. You are left with the time available to you for study and for other work related to law school. Any time left over is available to you for nonessential, non-law school related, activity.

This might all seem a little clinical to you. Surely I'm not telling you to plan your life for the next three years down to the second, and that there isn't any time for spontaneity and spur-of-the-moment decisions. Am I really suggesting that your life should be run on some sort of exaggerated conveyor-belt process, with only a certain amount of time for each activity before you move on to the next? Will you have to tell your son that you can spend 20.7 minutes playing catch before you spend 2 minutes traveling to your study where you will commence 3.2 hours of study for tomorrow's classes, so he should get his baseball glove and stopwatch and you can have some carefully timed fun?

No, that's not at all what I'm suggesting. My point here is that the amount of time you can devote to law school is *limited*. It's unrealistic to assume that you will come to law school and spend fourteen hours a day studying; there are just too many other things you need to do during the course of the day to make that a daily goal (although there might be some times in the semester when that amount of commitment is necessary). If you come to law school with that goal in mind and fail to accomplish it, you might not have a good sense of how to proceed. Worse still, you might become despondent and stop trying to get all of your work done. That can quickly lead you to a point where it's impossible to recover, meaning that you won't do as well in law school as you could or should. Better to know yourself as well as possible, set some realistic goals—based on your schedule and who you are—and try to meet those goals.

Knowing how much time it takes for you to be you also lets you be flexible. If you get off track with your studying one weekend, for example, you'll know how much time it will take you to get back on track and from where you might be able to get that time. Far from restricting your ability to be spontaneous, knowing how much time it takes to do the things you need to do can free you up to do some things you hadn't planned to do and still let you be successful in law school.

8

Writing

Reading about writing is much like reading about eating; the words mean something on an intellectual level, but a vital part of the experience is missing. Because you will be spending a considerable amount of time in law school studying legal writing, I am not going to take up too much space in an extensive discussion about the writing process. I think there a few aspects of writing that we can and should cover here, though, because there are things you can do before you come to law school to improve your writing skills.

One important point before I begin. Writing is an intensely personal subject and involves a lot of personal taste. I can only write about my thoughts, and I don't presume to suggest here that I offer a set of universal truths that everyone accepts. When it comes to writing, there are no such truths, and there are precious few rules as well.

Your professors will almost certainly be trying get you to write in a particular way. That's because they're trying to introduce you to a new style of writing—a new genre with which you're not yet familiar. That genre has certain established, almost cultural expectations about style and structure, and you'll spend a lot of time on those expectations in class. What they will be doing is working with you to make sure that your writing style is "correct" according to legal genre expectations. After that, it will be up to you to decide for yourself what "good" writing is within the confines of those expectations.

A. The General Perception That Lawyers Are Bad Writers

If you are honest, you probably don't have a very good opinion of lawyers as writers. You're not alone—my very subjective impression is that most people think lawyers are horrible writers. They probably think that legal writing classes are designed to make you as bad and confusing a writer as possible, so that you'll clog up every document you write with Latin phrases and hopelessly opaque language that only other lawyers have a hope of understanding.

People have been criticizing legal writing for centuries, and with good reason. As a profession, we seemed to celebrate—almost revel in—bad writing until quite recently. All those legal documents, with impenetrable phrases like "the party of the first part" and words like "hereinafter" and "testamentrix," not to mention the Latin, Old French, and antiquated English terms that seem to infect the law, are eloquent testimony to the way lawyers used to abuse language.

I say "used to," even though many lawyers are still bad writers, because things are changing. You will almost certainly not be taught in law school how to write in that dreadful, opaque style that many associate with lawyers. Instead, your legal writing teachers will probably work with you to promote a clean, simple, and direct writing style. You will be writing in formal English, of course, but in plain English and not the convoluted, difficult-to-understand style you might have expected.

Before we talk about the specifics of that writing style, I give you some quick words of warning. No matter how hard you work at developing a clear, simple, and accurate writing style, many people—including many judges and senior lawyers—are prejudiced against you. They think that lawyers in general are poor writers and that people of younger generations than they have particularly weak writing skills. It's important for you to put this prejudice in context. As far as I've been able to tell, each generation thinks the next generation is less literate, less skilled, and less talented than the one that came before it. Lawyers of my generation criticized the writing skills of the following generation, and both they and we are critical of your generation's writing skills. In a few years, you will have the opportunity to join the game and be critical of the next generation, and so on. Don't feel bad; my teachers criticized the sloppy writing of my cohorts, their teachers criticized them, their teachers criticized them, and so on back through time. If our writing was as bad as everyone before us seemed to think it was, we would surely have become illiterate by now, devolving back into communication by caveman grunts.

In fact, there are good and weak writers in every generation and each definable subgroup. Lawyers are no exception to this rule, and for anyone to lump all law students of their generation together and assume that all are poor writers is simply foolish. You can't control how anyone else feels, so don't waste energy trying. All you can do is write as well as you can, incorporating the lessons you learn in law school into your personal style of expression. Do that, and whatever bad things a person thinks about your generation as a whole, they won't think them about you.

What makes for "good" legal writing? Whatever your legal writing professor says about writing, of course, is the best gauge, but legal writing professors as a group would probably agree on some fundamental concepts: good legal writing is reader-centered, is easy to read, is not easy to write, and is ultimately about the character of the writer. Let's talk about each of these points in more detail.

B. Good Writing Is Reader-Centered

Good legal writing is more about the reader than the writer and is a discussion in which both talk to each other while the writer tries to inform the reader about a point of law. My word choice might strike you as odd: "discussion" implies a conversation between two people and "talk" suggests that we will be speaking to each other. Neither of these appear to be correct, because I am writing something at one time that you will read at some later time. We won't physically speak to each other, and without that personal give-and-take, it would seem to be impossible that we will be having a discussion.

But that's exactly what should be happening. As the writer, I should be conscious that you, as active readers, will be questioning my text. I should be anticipating those questions and trying to answer them, either structurally—by writing something that I know will provoke a question and then answering that question in the next block of text—or substantively, by anticipating your questions before you pose them and rewriting my work so that it answers them before they are asked.

The core concept in the word "discussion" is exchange. Discussion is an exchange of thoughts—a conversation, not two parallel monologues in which the participants express their own ideas but neither listen nor respond to the ideas of the other participant. We have all experienced that phenomenon—the experience of trying to speak with someone, only to realize that they're not interested in what we have to say and just want to tell us what they think. That isn't a conversation or a discussion—it's a speech.

By contrast, I hope we've all had the experience of a genuine discussion, a conversation in which each participant listens to the other person, reflects on what they have said, and responds to it. In this way, you can explore a topic's nuances and complexities, and both of you can feel the better for the experience. A true discussion involves a dialogue that can stimulate the mind in a way that being a passive listener to someone else's speech can't do.

When you encounter people who don't listen to anything you have to say and insist that you learn everything about what they think, you think of them as being self-centered. The same is true of writers who don't appear to be sensitive to the reader and what the reader needs to know. By contrast, writers who are considerate of the reader—who "listen" to the reader's questions and try to answer them—are reader-centered. That leads to one of my maxims of good legal writing: *good writing is reader-centered.*

As a writer, you have to spend a lot of time thinking about what you want to say and why you want to say it, of course, but you should spend at least as much time thinking about what your reader might be thinking about what you write and why the reader is participating in this dialogue. "I have to write this because I was told to" isn't really a satisfying reason for writing something, and neither is thinking that readers are reading your work because they have to—because they are senior attorneys, judges, or even legal writing teachers. The reader might have to read what you write, but there is hardly ever a requirement that he or she enjoy the process. Speaking as one who reads a lot for a living, I promise you that you want the reader to enjoy the experience. The best way to accomplish this is to take the reader into account when you write.

The easiest way to do this is to imagine to whom you are writing—someone you know and whose reactions you can predict. It's best if you can imagine a friend or family member who is intelligent but not a specialist in the area in which you're writing. That type of reader will be engaged with what you write—they want to learn what you have to say because they know and like you and because they are interested in learning what you want to tell them. Because they're not specialists in this area, they will have many questions. If you were having a face-to-face conversation, you can imagine that this person would interrupt you at key moments and ask you to explain your point. Your conversation wouldn't be linear, it would be recursive, just like the way an active reader reads a text.

If you were planning for a conversation like this, you would probably think about what you were going to say and what questions you might expect from the other person. You might try to anticipate those questions and how you might forestall them by being more clear and by answering them before they were asked.

That is the same process as reader-centered writing, and you can see how imagining your ideal reader can help you predict and answer questions in your writing so that you deliver information to the reader exactly when the reader needs to receive it. This takes some time, but if you are willing to take the effort, it will make the writing process much easier for you. Your writing will be easier to read and understand, something your teachers and future employers will greatly appreciate.

C. Good Writing Is Easy to Read

One of the simplest ways of helping the reader enjoy the experience of reading your work is to make your writing easy to read. That, in turn, means you should spend a lot of time thinking about the mechanics of writing—technical accuracy, structure, tone, and word choice.

Note that I didn't say that good writing is *accurate* writing. Usually it is, but that isn't always the case; if you've ever read a book written in dialect like *Huckleberry Finn*, you know what I mean. Legal writing is very different from literary writing, of course, and we don't have the luxury of making the choices that were open to Mark Twain. However, there can be a place for intentional inaccuracy to make a point, even if it happens rarely. The point is that we should never be so blindly devoted to a rule—whether it be that our writing should be technically accurate, formally structured, delivered in a formal voice, or anything else—that we miss the chance to make our point more forcefully or compellingly by bending or breaking the rule.

Although the distinction might be lost during law school, and might not present itself in your professional career either, it's helpful and more accurate to think of technical accuracy as an element that makes writing easy to read, rather than as a goal in itself.

1. *Technical Accuracy*

That said, for your purposes as legal writers, technical accuracy is almost always crucial to your goal of making your writing easier for your reader. You don't want anything to distract your reader from the points you're trying to make, and you don't want to convey to your reader that you're less than a credible source of information. Imagine having a conversation with someone about a complicated issue who consistently mispronounces a key word in the discussion. Soon, all you would be able to hear is that mispronunciation. You would not be paying any attention to the point the other person was trying to make, even if you could understand what was being said. It would be very difficult for you to take the speaker seriously—if he or she cannot pronounce the word accurately, you might legitimately wonder if he or she has anything intelligent to say about the topic.

This might not be a fair perception on your part. Of course a person can have an intelligent point to make about a topic while still mispronouncing a word or (to bring this back to writing) misspelling one. But fairness is not a legitimate expectation when it comes to communication. Your reader might give you the benefit of the doubt if you make technical mistakes (misspelled words, incomplete sentences, inaccurate punctuation, and so on) in your work, but don't count on it. Remember that your words are the only thing the reader has to go on when forming an impression of your credibility. You are not standing in front of someone, able to persuade them by your appearance, your gestures, or your facial expressions that you are an intelligent and persuasive advocate. You appear only in the form of the words you have chosen to make your point and the way you have chosen to place those words in relation to one another.

2. Structure

Careful attention to structure is another element of writing that's easy to read. There are several structural elements for you to think about: the sentence, the paragraph, the section, and the ordering of different sections are the four that come readily to mind. You are certainly familiar with the first two, but it might have been a while since you gave careful thought to whether all the words in a sentence, for example, are organized as effectively as possible. I don't mean just on a formal level—whether you use active voice to convey information or passive voice to obscure a person's role in events, for example—but also on a subtler level. A good writer is always asking whether each word carries its weight in a sentence, whether another word would do a better job, whether one word follows another effectively, or whether its position in the sentence should be changed, and so on.

The good writer uses that same level of scrutiny on all the sentences in a paragraph. It's not enough that each word follows the previous word effectively, it's important that each sentence locks into the sentences around it to help make the paragraph as tight and controlled as possible. If analogies help, think of an idea as a gymnast and the paragraph as a floor: the floor can either be unresponsive, like a concrete slab, or sprung, like the equipment used in the floor exercise. A concrete floor supports the athletes' weight, but does nothing more. A sprung floor supports weight as well, of course, but it also helps propel the gymnasts, allowing them to perform at their best. A good paragraph can have the same effect on an idea—it can help it soar.

When all of these carefully structured sentences and sprung paragraphs are put together, they should form a tight section of a longer document. Sections should not be too long or too short, but should contain all (and only) the necessary information to make up a discrete part of a complete document. When strung together, those individual sections should make a coherent whole that accomplishes its purpose—to persuade, inform, entertain (although that isn't usually the primary goal of legal writers), or whatever purpose the writer had in mind.

3. *Voice*

Another crucial element to writing that's easy to read is *tone*—the voice you use to express yourself. A good writer spends a lot of time thinking carefully about tone in every piece of writing and will speak in several different voices depending on the subject under discussion and the context in which the reader will encounter the writing. This book, for instance, is (I hope) written in a somewhat casual and relaxed tone, very different from the voice I use when I write articles to be read by my academic colleagues, different from the voice I used for the informal pieces I wrote for clients or fellow lawyers when I was in practice, and very different from the voice in which I would write formal documents to be filed in court.

It isn't hard to keep these voices separate if you keep the context of the writing clearly in mind. Just as you wouldn't walk into court in a T-shirt and jeans and say "Hi judge. How're you doin'?", you won't—or shouldn't—write a sentence with contractions like "wouldn't," "won't," or "shouldn't" (or, shudder, "how're" or "doin'") when writing a formal document. Contractions are inherently informal and have no place in formal writing. Writing "Good morning ladies and gentlemen. I hope you are well this morning" as the start of an email you write to some close friends would be equally inappropriate. Context is everything.

Remember: just as body language conveys a great deal about you without saying anything, the voice you choose to convey written meaning can carry important encoded messages to the reader. Consider the following two fictitious emails:

> Professor X,
> My notes from class reflect that you said that duty is not an element of the tort of negligence. My classmates tell me that you said that duty is an element of this tort. The textbook appears to support their position.
> Please inform me as to who is correct at your earliest convenience.
> Student One

> Hi Professor,
> Well, I seem to be really confused today! I was reviewing my notes from today's class and I wrote down that duty isn't an element of negligence, but when I was talking to a few of my friends they told me that I'd gotten it wrong and that duty is an element. I reread the textbook and it looks pretty clear that I got it wrong in class, but I was hoping you could just confirm that I misheard you.

Sorry to bother you! Thanks for your help.
Student Two

If asked to characterize the tone of these two messages, I would say the first sounds formal and angry, whereas the second sounds relaxed and cheerful. It might well be that Student One didn't intend to sound angry, but if that is the case, the student either wasn't listening closely enough to the voice he or she was using to communicate or the student is tone-deaf, which is a serious condition for those of us who spend our lives communicating in writing. Clearly, though, Student Two intended to sound relaxed and apologetic. It's not the tone of email you would choose for all situations—the use of exclamation marks, for example, would be inappropriate in a formal context but works well in an informal context to indicate that the writer is relaxed and intends that the reader should take no offense at what is being written—but the tone is well calculated to the context of this communication and is, I hope you agree, more effective than Student One's effort.

4. Plain Language

The last feature of easy-to-read writing is plain language, a topic that is often misunderstood. "Plain language," as I use the phrase here and as we generally use it in law school, means words that tend to be simple and in English. That doesn't mean that there is anything wrong with complex or non-English words, just that—generally speaking—their use makes writing less easy to understand than their simple, English counterparts.

If you doubt me, consider this: "Operosian scriveners' verisimilitudanal bona fides can remain opaque when they employ an occupational argot." That's a contrived and intentionally bad sentence (although it doesn't use unreasonably complex vocabulary), that means, in essence, "it's hard to tell if hard-working writers are telling the truth when they use jargon." Which sentence was easier to understand, even if you knew the meaning of all the words in both? Because the meaning of both sentences are essentially the same, what benefit does a writer gain by using the harder-to-understand words, other than demonstrating the depth of his or her vocabulary? Showing off isn't a laudable trait.

As for using English, it only seems polite to the reader for a writer to use a country's conventional language. Although it might be true that "Was mich nicht umbringt, macht mich stärker," it's probably better to translate Nietzsche as saying "that which does not kill me makes me stronger." At least we have a shared basis for a conversation on whether we agree with the sentiment. Of course, you might read German fluently, in which case, the translation would be unnecessary. I, as the writer here, don't know that for certain, and I cannot assume that all of you speak that language (even assuming that I can speak it, which in my case would be a stretch). I would be introducing an unfair obstacle in the path of your understanding if I wrote in it.

You should note that my insistence on plain English doesn't limit one to the language or intellectual level of kindergarten. For one thing, foreign words—like *kindergarten*—that have been assimilated into English are fair game for plain English usage. Even the most complicated thought can be expressed in simple words—it's the complexity of the thought that's important, not the complexity of the language expressing it. If you doubt me, read the U.S. Constitution sometime. The framers of that document were able to generate an administrative and philosophical blueprint for this country that has lasted for over 200 years, and the vocabulary they used is relatively simple and plain, even to us who read it today.

As you prepare to study legal writing, think about what you are reading and ask if the writer has taken the trouble to express him or herself in technically accurate, thoughtfully structured, plain English. If so, I'll bet you found it easy to read. Whether or not you agreed with the writer is a different question, of course.

D. Good Writing Is Not Easy

You might have noticed that I said the writer had "taken trouble" in the previous paragraph, and that's a phrase I used intentionally. Good writing that's easy to read is hardly ever easy to write. Rather, it takes some time and effort to generate a document that's focused on the reader and has no technical, structural, or linguistic blemishes that impede easy understanding of the points it contains. Good writing, in short, is a pain to write.

If you are one of those people who can write clear, simple, polished prose in one draft, I envy you. I also think you're deluding yourself—no one can write at their very best in one draft. Most people take multiple drafts to write serviceable prose, and there's nothing wrong with that. You might be impressed with the way a musician plays a piece during a concert, but you don't hear the months of practice that went into mastering the technical difficulties the piece presented. Though you might be impressed by a piece of writing that seems graceful and effortless, you haven't seen the numerous drafts the writer went through before finally publishing it.

Even if you have done well in your previous academic career by leaving your writing to the last second, claiming that you "write better under pressure," now is the time to reconsider that strategy. Maybe you have done well up until now, but law school is full of students who have done well in their academic careers. In fact, there is not one person in your law school class who isn't highly intelligent and didn't perform at the highest level all the way through the educational system. Those who do well in law school are willing to go beyond what has worked for them in the past and will work harder and smarter than before. As far as writing is concerned, the single best thing you can do to improve your writing is to commit to writing at least two more drafts of your work than you have prepared in the past. If you do that, and if you try to make real improvements with each draft, you will almost certainly do better than you would have done without the additional drafts.

E. Good Writing Is About Character

If I had to sum up everything I think about writing into one phrase, it would be this: good writing is about character. Let me take a couple of paragraphs to explain this.

What I have said about writing in this section should lead you to the conclusion that I think good writing is about caring for the reader. I've said that in my opinion, good writing is reader-centered, that the writer should take trouble to make documents easy to read, and that good writing takes a lot of work. All of that work, on behalf of a reader that you probably will not know, suggests that you are willing to put yourself out to make sure that the reader benefits from reading your work. One way to describe someone who works hard to help others is as a person of good character.

It's true, of course, that a good person behaves well without the expectation of reward, whereas lawyers are writing for clients and are paid for their efforts. The better the work, the more they will be paid for it. This doesn't change my perception of the relationship between good writing and character, because lawyers don't have to take the trouble to write well, they just need to be functional writers. Those who take the trouble to write documents that are better than just functional display the traits of good character that will help them become better writers.

I should be clear that the obverse of this position is not correct—bad writing is definitely *not* a sign of bad character. Bad writing can exist for many reasons, but hardly any of them involve a desire to write badly. No rational law student or lawyer, given the choice between writing well and writing badly, would choose to write badly. Although good writing is almost always associated with good character, bad writing has multiple causes.

As you think about writing something—anything—think about how your reader will perceive your document. Have you adopted a tone that's appropriate for the point you want to make (conversational, formal, relaxed, rigid, angry, cheerful, etc.)? Have you chosen the best words to convey your point? Have you organized the words effectively into tight sentences, well-constructed paragraphs, and carefully arranged sections? Have you edited your work (even emails should be edited) to make sure it is accurate, uses an appropriate voice for the message you're trying to convey, and is in appropriately plain language? If you have done these things, your reader might not appreciate how much trouble you've gone to, but he or she will know that the document is easy to read. Almost every reader appreciates that, and you'll be a good person to have gone to that trouble.

This all takes time, so don't worry if the documents you generate at the start of your law school career aren't perfect. The important thing is to try to make your documents as well written as possible. If you keep that in mind, progress will come quickly. Even if it comes more slowly than you would like, you'll be displaying a great deal of character as you engage in the process.

> **Exercise:** Try incorporating the ideas expressed in this chapter to every-thing you write for anyone other than yourself to read. Even if what you are writing is a simple email, ask yourself if the point you are making could be expressed better, more simply, and in plainer, more technically accurate English.
>
> Try to write every day, even if you write a journal recording the events of your day. Imagine that a future biographer wants to know about you, and think about how what you are writing would convey information to that person. Would your reader think of you as a technically skilled writer? Would your reader like you? Does that matter to you, as long as the events are accurately recorded? Try different drafts to vary your tone, compare the different drafts to each other, and think carefully about every word, phrase, and sentence in your journal entry. Are they as well chosen as possible?
>
> Try writing several drafts about an event and indicating to the reader that you are happy about the event in one draft and unhappy in the other, not by your word choice but by the voice you use to express yourself.
>
> Do this every day and you will quickly become a better writer.

9

Structure of the U.S. Court System

Your critical reading skills should be finely honed enough for you to mistrust any short piece of writing that claims to treat something as complex as the structure of the multiple court systems in this country. Clearly, that topic is much too large to be covered in a brief overview and any chapter that makes such a claim can only contain a very cursory overview at best.

That's exactly what this chapter is: a very cursory overview of the U.S. court system. In the next few pages we'll talk about some of the federal Article III courts (so-called because they're authorized by Article III of the Constitution. There are other types of federal court, collectively known as Article I courts), and we'll talk about a generalized, nonspecific state court system. You will learn more specifically about the various state court systems at law school, but that's more information than you need right now. Then we discuss the relationship between state and federal courts—when their work intersects and when it doesn't. This is important for you to know, because it might affect how you read the decisions from those courts.

A. Federal Courts

It's difficult to write anything about any court system without including the disclaimer that there are exceptions to any general statement you make. So it is with the federal court system. A general statement that there are three levels to the system—trial court, intermediate appellate court, and Supreme Court—is partially true. This statement ignores, among other things, the Article I courts presided over by U.S. magistrate judges, bankruptcy judges, and other trial courts; the appellate jurisdiction of district courts over some matters tried by some Article I courts; and the Supreme Court's original jurisdiction over some matters. Attempting to cover all the possible permutations of court jurisdiction and structure would take a book all by itself, and much of this you likely will cover in your civil procedure course in law school. For now, almost anything I say about the federal courts here will have exceptions to it. I try to indicate that by writing "usually" or "in most cases" or some other escape language.

1. Civil versus Criminal

There is a threshold matter to discuss before getting to court structure, and that is the difference between civil and criminal matters.

The difference between cases involving civil damages and criminal penalties is that while both can involve money (one can be ordered to pay a fine in a criminal case, and ordered to pay restitution as well), only criminal cases can involve the deprivation of a person's liberty. Put simply, you can be put in jail for some crimes, but you cannot be put in jail for a case involving civil damages.

Note that civil cases do not have to involve money. In fact, as you will learn, there is a whole branch of civil law concerned with compelling or preventing behavior in which money plays, at best, only a collateral role. This is *equity*, an important area of civil law. If you want to stop a fast food restaurant chain from discriminating against African Americans, for instance, you might sue the chain in equity and seek an injunction that forces it to engage in some behavior (racial sensitivity training for its employees, for example) and prevent it from engaging in other behavior (not serving African Americans for long periods of time while other customers are served more rapidly, for example).

Initiating and following through on such a program would, of course, be very expensive for the restaurant chain, which is why I say that money plays a collateral role in equitable relief. You cannot ignore the fact that there will be costs associated with the relief sought by the plaintiff, but the plaintiff isn't the one asking for the money. Defendants sometimes don't appreciate that difference, because regardless of how the form of relief is couched by the courts, the bottom line is that a loss will cost them lots of money. For lawyers, the distinctions between law and equity are very important. By contrast, if you've been the victim of the restaurant chain's discrimination and want money damages as a result, you would bring a suit for legal damages. You will explore the complex and fascinating relationship between law and equity much more thoroughly in your civil procedure class.

We use different words to describe the findings of civil and criminal juries. In criminal cases, the defendant is "guilty" or "not guilty." In civil cases, the defendant is "liable" or "not liable." There are other important distinctions between civil and criminal cases as well, most notably the burden of proof, which is "beyond a reasonable doubt" in criminal cases and "by a preponderance of the evidence" or "clear and convincing" in civil cases. The rules governing how these cases proceed are also different, and criminal cases take scheduling priority over civil cases because of the requirement that a criminal defendant get a speedy trial.

2. Trial Court Level

Most federal trials—either civil or criminal—happen at the district court level. Every state has at least one federal district court with several district judges associated with it. Many states have more than one district, some with separate divisions within them. These are administrative conveniences that allow judges to share centralized clerking and other administrative services, although you will want to consider the potential legal effect of these divisions when considering venue and jurisdiction in your civil procedure classes.

One quick word about jurisdiction, because it's important for you to know what types of cases these federal trial courts can hear. Federal courts are courts of limited jurisdiction, meaning that they can only hear the cases that the Constitution and federal statutes allow them to hear. This can get complicated, especially in certain parts of the country. If you are given a speeding ticket, for example, you're not likely to go to federal court to challenge it, even if you get that ticket on an interstate highway. But if you get a speeding ticket on some roads, you might have to go to federal court because the road runs through a federal reservation, and enforcing the driving laws falls under federal jurisdiction.

For present purposes, though, let's keep things simple. If there is a federal statute covering some behavior—criminal or civil—then the trial court proceedings concerning that behavior can be heard by the federal district court. Sometimes the district judge will hear the entire proceedings without a jury. This is called a bench trial and is sometimes required by statute or requested by the parties. More often, though, the judge will empanel a jury to listen to the facts of the case and issue a verdict or findings. The judge always makes decisions about the law.

In addition to federal criminal law cases and cases that involve federal civil law, the federal district courts can also hear cases involving state civil law under special circumstances. This has important ramifications when we consider the hierarchy of authority, something we will do after the overview of the federal court system.

The federal district courts sometimes publish their opinions, usually in the *Federal Supplement* reporter for cases written by federal district court judges.

These days, court opinions are available from a lot of Internet sources as well—either databases that charge a fee, like Westlaw and Lexis, or free databases, such as the court's own Web site. We talk more about the publishing question in the next section, devoted to the federal intermediate appellate courts—the Courts of Appeals.

3. The Courts of Appeals

Once the federal district court is finished with a civil case, and assuming the parties didn't settle the dispute, the losing party can appeal. In criminal cases, the defendant can appeal if convicted at trial. The government does not get to appeal if the defendant is acquitted, because of the Constitution's protection against double jeopardy. In the federal court system, that appeal usually goes to the relevant Circuit Court of Appeals.

There are eleven numbered circuits, as well as the Court of Appeals for the District of Columbia. Each circuit has jurisdiction over the federal district courts located in several states but not—and this is crucially important and frequently misunderstood by law students—over the state courts in those states. Remember that we're only speaking about federal courts at the moment, so when you learn that, for example, the Second Circuit has jurisdiction over the federal district courts in New York, don't assume that this means the Second Circuit also has jurisdiction over the New York state court system, or that Second Circuit decisions have special precedential value to New York's state courts. As a strictly legal matter, they don't. This doesn't mean that the state court won't pay attention to what the federal court might have said about its law.

You will learn much more about this when you cover the hierarchy of authority, but for now remember this: just because a federal district court is located physically within a state, that doesn't mean that it has influence over the state courts in that state. The physical location of a federal court might have some implications for the federal court, but, as a matter of law, it rarely has much importance to the state court.

You might think that the Courts of Appeals aren't that important, because they're the intermediate appellate courts; they sit between the trial court, where the facts and the law are hashed out in the familiar litigation atmosphere that we've all seen in courtroom dramas, and the United States Supreme Court, that august body whose every pronouncement seems to be headline news. The Courts of Appeals might seem like way-stations, transitory points on the way from trial court drama to jurisprudential history. This is an inaccurate view.

The Courts of Appeals are the last stop for almost every piece of contested litigation in the federal system. The Supreme Court has never heard many cases during its court year, and these days it's hearing even fewer cases each year. The bottom line is that the chances of having a case going to the Supreme Court are so slim that the vast majority of lawyers in this country who spend their careers litigating cases in federal court will never argue or even work on a case that gets there. For almost everyone, the Courts of Appeals are the practical (if not theoretical) courts of last resort.

That makes them incredibly important to the federal court system, and it makes their announced decisions highly significant. Like the federal district courts, though, they have limited jurisdiction; they can only hear the cases they are permitted to hear by the Constitution or statute. That keeps them very busy, and the volume of cases has an effect on how they hear the cases.

Each Circuit Court of Appeals has a certain number of active judges sitting, as well as a number of senior judges. Article III judges have constitutionally protected jobs. They can't be fired for any reason, they can only be impeached, and that hardly ever happens. Once a judge reaches a certain age, combined with a certain number of years of service as a federal judge, he or she can become a senior judge. That might mean that the judge stops hearing cases completely, stops coming to the courthouse, and, in effect, retires. Senior judges continue to be paid, but do not have to do anything. A senior judge can continue hearing the same number of cases as before or can take a reduced schedule—it's entirely up to the judge. Senior judges don't count when tallying up the number of judges sitting on the Circuit Court, though—that's limited to active judges. The political process being what it is, every Circuit Court has some vacancies that haven't been filled while the nominees go through the approval process. How long that takes, and why some nominees are delayed for years while others fly through the process, is a subject for another time and place; you might want to do some reading on your own if you're interested.

Cases are usually assigned to a panel of three judges for a hearing, but a case might not always have three active judges on the panel. Senior judges can be added to panels, as can any Article III judge who can be asked to sit "by designation." When you look at the list of judges who decided a case, see if there any indications that the judge was sitting by designation; that might be relevant to your class discussion or, later, to the attorneys with whom you work.

Once the panel has considered the case—often after oral argument, although these days oral argument is becoming rarer as courts try to conserve their time and resources by considering more cases on the briefs filed by the parties—it will have a conference where it makes an initial decision about who should win the appeal and why. The active judge in the majority with the most seniority assigns the case to one of the panel judges to write the decision. If there is an oral argument in the case, this conference often comes minutes after the argument is over.

Once the designated judge writes a draft opinion in the case—and this can take many months if the case is complicated—the draft circulates among the panel members (and, in some circuits, perhaps to the other circuit judges as well) and if a panel member disagrees strongly enough with the decision or the way it was reached, he or she might write a dissent that is also circulated. It can happen that another panel member becomes convinced that the dissent is more persuasive than the proposed majority opinion and switches votes. If that happens, the dissent becomes the majority (it's only a three-judge panel, so the change of one vote from the majority to the dissent makes all the difference). Sometimes the judge who wrote the opinion that was originally planned as the majority decision might rework it to become a dissent.

After all that behind-the-scenes wrangling is over, the court issues its opinion. The parties then have some choices. The losing party on appeal can either accept the court's decision, in which case the litigation is over, or it can ask the panel to reconsider its decision. That usually happens if the panel has made an obvious, but important, mistake (if the panel thought that a certain fact had been established at trial, for example, when the record shows that the fact was not established). The losing party can also ask for a rehearing, which happens not with the three-judge panel but in front of all the judges on that particular Circuit Court of Appeals. This type of hearing—known as an *en banc* review—typically doesn't happen often (maybe once or twice a year) but must be quite an experience for the lawyers who participate in it. Questions can come from any and all of the judges who are sitting behind such a long bench that it must seem as if the lawyer is literally surrounded by questioners.

The other alternative a losing party has, of course, is to ask the Supreme Court to review the case—and "ask" is the crucial word here. Although anyone who loses at trial has the right to appeal the case to the Court of Appeals, almost no one has the right to ask the Supreme Court to hear a case. Instead, the losing party on appeal has to file a legal request know as a petition seeking a writ of certiorari with the Supreme Court, explaining the reasons why it should hear the case. These petitions, known informally as "cert. petitions," are much more frequently denied than accepted, but the fact that the Supreme Court has decided not to hear a case can be relevant to lawyers and courts, so you sometimes see the words "cert. denied" following a case citation. Usually those words will be accompanied by a citation of their own. Sometimes the Supreme Court says it won't hear a case but gives some reasons for its decision. Lawyers can sometimes glean helpful information from the Court's explanation.

Decisions from the various courts of appeals are typically reproduced in the *Federal Reporter*, which has run through both the first and second series and is now into the third series. These are indicated by the citation "F.," "F.2d" (for second series), and F.3d (third series). Things get a little complicated when we speak of "publication" when it comes to Courts of Appeals decisions.

As with the federal district courts, Courts of Appeals decisions can be found in a number of places in addition to the book-style reporters published by West; they are in computer databases such as Lexis and Westlaw, as well as other for-profit legal databases and not-for-profit ones, such as the court Web sites. Some "unpublished" Courts of Appeals decisions are also published in the *Federal Appendix*, a book type reporter series. Now if you were reading carefully and actively, that last sentence should have brought you up short: how can an "unpublished" decision be "published" somewhere? It's a fair question, and one that many people asked when the *Federal Appendix* first began publication.

The problem, of course, is that it's very difficult to say that anything is "unpublished" when it's readily available, yet the Courts of Appeals used to have rules forbidding lawyers from citing their unpublished decisions. This has been a topic of heated debate over the past few years, and reasonable people can (and have) differed over why these policies were in place and whether they were a good idea. As with so many things discussed here, you might be interested in following up on this debate and reading more about it. I don't get into the merits of the courts' publication policy here, except to say that the courts claim that "unpublished" decisions deal with issues of law that are settled and uncontroversial, and that they might be written and analyzed with less careful attention to detail than would appear in their published decisions.

Referring to a decision as "unpublished" is clearly inaccurate when it *is* published and readily available in any number of online and print sources. Courts began instead to speak of "precedential" and "nonprecedential" opinions, and that's probably a better way of looking at them, although thinking of decisions in this way can be a little misleading. The deciding court cannot really decide whether its decision is binding on someone else, because that decision can only be made by the later court that looks at what the previous court wrote and decides for itself whether to follow it. It's also true that a Second Circuit opinion is not, for example, precedential in the Fourth Circuit, in the Supreme Court, or in any state court. Thinking of a decision as "precedential" can cause some problems if you don't think carefully through the implications of the word.

We will talk more about the importance of precedential and nonprecedential, or published and nonpublished decisions when we cover hierarchy of authority. For now, though, look at the citation of the case: if it has "F.," "F.2d," or "F.3d" in it, then it's precedential or published, and that includes a citation that looks like this: "___ F.3d ___." You probably will not see that in your textbooks, but you might see it in cases once you start doing legal research. It means that the case will be published in the *Federal Reporter*, but it was decided so recently that the publisher hasn't decided what volume it will be in or on what page). If, on the other hand, the case citation only has "slip op." or F. (or Fed.) App'x), "WL" or "LEXIS," then the decision is probably unpublished or nonprecedential.

The bottom line is that you should understand the nature of every opinion you read, and you can do that first by looking at the citation. For every case— whether in your law school textbook, given to you as part of a legal writing assignment, or found by you as part of your research—you should figure out from which court the opinion comes and what its precedential value might be. This is something that becomes instinctive over time, but it takes a lot of work to begin with. Put the work in, though; you will be better prepared and will do better in law school if you do.

4. *The Supreme Court*

The Supreme Court is an extraordinarily important institution. There is no way to minimize the significance of the Court, symbolized by the fact that we typically use a capital "C" in "Court" when we write about it—the only other time you do that is when you're writing to a specific court: "In *Smith*, this Court held that…." If you write "In *Smith*, the Court held that….", the difference between "this" and "the" means that you're writing about the Supreme Court in the second example.

The people who sit on the Court aren't even called judges. Rather, they are "justices," and woe betide anyone who forgets it. Although the justices are sometimes irreverently referred to as "the Supremes," no one should ever forget that they are an extremely important group of men and women whose decisions have direct effects on the way we live our lives.

Before we fall over ourselves in reverence, though, remember that the Supreme Court, like all federal courts, has limited jurisdiction. Although the Court is often referred to as "the highest court in the land," that's not quite true. It's correct to think of the Court as being the highest court for all federal and constitutional questions that make their way through the courts, but the Supreme Court doesn't have the final word on questions of state law— that is reserved for the highest court in the state court system where the law in question was promulgated. Although the Supreme Court, for example, can tell New Mexico what to do if New Mexico's laws contravene the Constitution, and it can tell the federal district court located in New Mexico what to do about questions of federal law, it cannot tell the New Mexico Supreme Court what to do about a matter that arises purely under the laws of New Mexico.

This a distinction that's often lost on nonlawyers, who think of the Supreme Court simply as the most important court there is. This is a mistake you cannot afford to make. There is no question that anything the Supreme Court says about anything is important, but it's not all equally important. When the Court has jurisdiction over something, and when it's writing specifically about those matters, no court is more important. But if the Court is reflecting about something and comments that it doesn't like a state's law, that opinion is no more binding on the state court than yours or mine. The Court's opinion might be more influential than other federal courts' decisions, perhaps, and certainly more newsworthy, but not binding.

One reflection of the Supreme Court's importance is that fact that every decision it hands down is published, both in the physical and precedential senses: there are no unpublished or nonprecedential Supreme Court decisions. In fact, the decisions are published in not one but three different reporters; the *United States Reports*, published by the Court itself, the *Supreme Court Reporter*, published by West, and the *Lawyer's Edition*. These are abbreviated, for citation purposes, as "U.S.," "S.Ct.," and "L.Ed.," and you'll often see citations to all three reporters in citations to the Court's decisions, although that isn't correct formal citation form, as you will discover when you discuss citations in class.

The Supreme Court has nine justices who all hear every case, unless one of them has a potential conflict of interest and recuses him or herself. As with the Courts of Appeals, the Court will typically issue an opinion explaining its decision and, if one or more of the justices dissents from the majority opinion, each or all can write a dissenting opinion as well. Justices might also write an opinion concurring in the judgment, which usually means that they agree with the decision itself but they disagree on how the majority reached its decision.

This can make things complicated, because sometimes a result will have a majority, but the rationale used in reaching that result will not. Assume there's a case in which three justices agree on the result and on the way the result should be reached. Two additional justices agree on the result but each write concurring opinions explaining that they would reach the decision in different ways from each other and from the three justices who agreed on everything. Four justices disagree with the result and the Court's rationale and write their own, dissenting opinion. In this situation, the largest voting bloc is, ironically, in the minority, and there's no majority that agrees on how the result should be reached. This is known as a plurality decision. Law school professors love pluralities because they allow us to explore many different nuances in the facts and law of a case. Keep an eye out for these cases in your textbooks, and when you see them, be prepared to answer questions about the differing analyses offered by the various justices. If your professor has assigned a case decided by a plurality, you will almost certainly have a lively conversation about the merits of the various positions adopted by the justices.

The Supreme Court reaches its decisions after extensive briefing by the parties and sometimes by other interested groups or individuals who have an interest in the outcome of the case, even though they are not formally part of the lawsuit. The briefs filed by these "friends of the Court," or *amici*, can be very valuable sources of research; if you are interested in a legal issue that's been argued before the Supreme Court, take a look at the briefs. They are available in some free Internet databases and on the commercial databases as well. Briefs for some of the most important Supreme Court cases are also available in book form.

You might be interested in listening to the oral argument of a particular case, although this is often of more historical interest than legal because after the Court issues its opinion, the issues discussed at oral argument become much less significant. Still, just as oral arguments can help judges and justices sharpen their understanding of an issue, listening to the justices grappling with difficult legal issues can help clarify why they later wrote their opinions. As with all other federal courts, the Supreme Court does not allow TV cameras to record its proceedings, but the audio recordings of many of the Court's most important recent arguments can be found online.

B. State Courts

Each state has its own court system that, broadly speaking, mimics the layout just discussed for the federal system. The names of the courts in each of the different state systems might be different, but typically they function either as trial courts, intermediate appellate courts, or high courts (also known as courts of last resort, or courts of final appeal).

You can tell you are reading a decision from a state court by looking at the citation. Some states publish their own official reporters, so if you see a citation with something that looks like a state abbreviation in it—123 Md. 456, for example—that tells you that the decision was published in the *Maryland Reports*, and that means that it's a decision from Maryland's highest court, the Court of Appeals of Maryland. It's important to remember that you cannot rely on court names to tell you much about the court. In Maryland, for example, the trial courts are called "Circuit Courts," which sounds a lot like the federal intermediate courts, the Circuit Courts of Appeals. The Maryland intermediate appellate court is the Court of Special Appeals, which sounds as if it might be the highest court because of the "special" nature of the appeals heard there, whereas the name "Court of Appeals" might make you think of the intermediate appellate court. In New York, the trial court system is known as the "Supreme Court," and the highest court is the "Court of Appeals." By contrast, in Iowa, the highest court is the "Supreme Court." The point is that until you become very secure in your understanding of which court is which, you will be safer checking up on the level of the court each time you read an opinion. You can find all the relevant information about court names in the *Bluebook* or the *ALWD Manual*.

All state court decisions are also published in one of the regional reporters, even those that are also published in the state's official reporter. Citations to these reporters have initials corresponding to various regions in them—N.E. for the *North Eastern Reporter*, S.W. for the *South Western Reporter*, and so on. Again, if you are not sure what reporter is being referred to by the citation, look it up in either the *Bluebook* or the *ALWD Manual*. It only takes a second, and it's very important to know which court issued the opinion. Law school textbooks will often make this simpler by giving you the name of the court, but sometimes the internal citations within a case aren't so straightforward. For example, if you are reading a decision you know comes from the Virginia Supreme Court, but read that the court relied on a decision identified as "*Smith v. Jones*, 123 A.2d 456 (Del. 1988)" you should realize on your own that the *Smith* decision comes from Delaware. The decision might make this clear, but it might not.

In general, you will only read opinions from a state's appellate courts because state trial court decisions are not thought to be important enough to publish. The value or importance of each decision is determined in at least three ways: first, by looking at the level of the court that issued the opinion; second, by determining the legal issue involved; and third, by looking at the context in which the opinion is going to be used. In other words, an opinion from a state's highest court is typically more important than an opinion from the state's intermediate appellate court, but neither might have much importance if you cite to them to support a position you're asserting in a different state or in federal court. As with many other things in life, context is everything. We explore the importance of context and hierarchy in the next chapter. For now, here's an exercise that can help you think about court systems.

Exercise: Each day, find a newspaper reference to a court. Find out as much as you can about the court. Is it a state court or federal court? What level of court is it? Do some research if necessary to find out where the court is located and anything else that appears to be relevant. Reread the news story once you have found out as much as you can. Consider whether the information you have learned helps you understand the story better, or whether you can spot some mistakes in the way the reporter has written the story that you might not otherwise have detected.

10

Hierarchy of Authority

Understanding what a court is—federal or state, trial level or appellate—can be helpful information when understanding what the court has done. Understanding where a court stands in the hierarchy of authority is crucial for you as law students and as lawyers. The sooner you learn how to understand how to locate a particular case in the hierarchy, the better you will understand where that case fits in the complex web of authority.

There are a lot of things for you to consider when locating a case in the hierarchy of authority. It's not enough to say that one court ranks higher than another court; you also have to know the legal issue involved, and whether this court can speak with authority on that issue. We cover these considerations in turn.

A. Court Ranking

As with many things in the law, this area has a clear rule and then a much fuzzier gray area that requires some interpretation. At the beginning of your law school career, it's sensible for you to focus more on the clear rule and keep the gray area in the back of your mind.

The good thing about this particular rule is that it's easily stated: courts can only bind those courts directly below them in the hierarchy of authority. Simple. What it means is hardly more complicated.

As you know, in the federal system there are three layers of courts; trial (district courts), intermediate appellate (Courts of Appeals), and ultimate (the Supreme Court). Each Court of Appeals has responsibility for a particular set of jurisdictions; the Second Circuit, for example, covers the federal district courts located in Vermont, Connecticut, and New York. Sometimes, states are big enough to have more than one federal district located within them: Connecticut and Vermont, for example, are relatively small states and each only has one federal district, whereas New York is a large state and has four districts—the Northern, Southern, Eastern, and Western districts.

Some diagrams might help make this clearer. Figure 1 shows the hierarchy of authority within the Courts of Appeals.

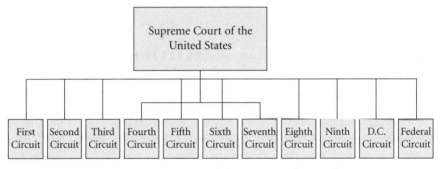

Figure 1. Hierarchy of the Courts of Appeals.

Figure 2 is a diagram that shows the hierarchy of authority within the Second Circuit.

The Supreme Court is at the top, of course, because it's the highest federal court. Then come each of the Courts of Appeals, each aligned at the same level. Below each Court of Appeals come the various district courts.

Now it's easy to see what the rule means. The Supreme Court binds all the federal courts, because they are below it in the hierarchy of authority. Each

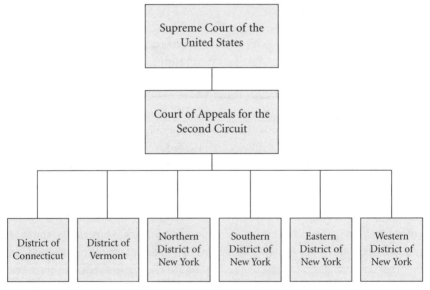

Figure 2. Second Circuit Hierarchy of Courts.

Court of Appeals binds all the district courts that fall below it in the hierarchy of authority; in the example in Figure 2, Second Circuit decisions bind the district courts of Connecticut, Vermont, and New York. But Second Circuit decisions don't, for example, bind the Fourth Circuit because the Fourth Circuit doesn't fall below the Second Circuit. Fourth Circuit decisions don't bind the district court of Vermont, because the Fourth Circuit isn't aligned directly above Vermont. District court opinions don't bind any other courts, because no one is below them in the hierarchy of authority.

The same rule applies when looking at state court hierarchies. The highest courts of the various states are all aligned in a row, like the Courts of Appeal, and the intermediate appellate courts and trial courts of each state are aligned below the relevant highest court. So the Court of Appeals of Maryland, for example, binds the Maryland intermediate appellate court (the Court of Special Appeals) and the Maryland trial courts (the Circuit Courts), but not any of the courts in, for example, the New York court system.

This is what you would expect from a country in which states' rights are extraordinarily important. Each state has authority over its own laws, and no state court can bind any the courts of any other state. Things get a little more complicated, though, when federal courts consider state law and when the Constitution comes into play.

B. Legal Issues

As courts of limited jurisdiction, federal courts can only hear those cases the Constitution or Congress has authorized them to hear. Under certain circumstances, that means that federal courts can hear issues of state law. When they do, the rule stays the same—a lower court is bound by the decisions of the courts aligned directly above it—but the identity of the players changes a little.

Once again, a chart might help explain this. Let's suppose that a district court in the Northern District of New York hears a case under the laws of Maryland. Figure 3 shows what the hierarchy of authority looks like now.

This probably looks like heresy: the Supreme Court is now down on the same level as the trial court and the Court of Appeals, and the two state courts are aligned directly above the federal trial court. If I had included all the other federal Courts of Appeals, they would be on the same line as the Second Circuit and the Supreme Court. Remember, we're dealing with a question of state law now, and the state courts are the only ones who get to say what state law is (with one important exception that we'll get to in a second). And remem-

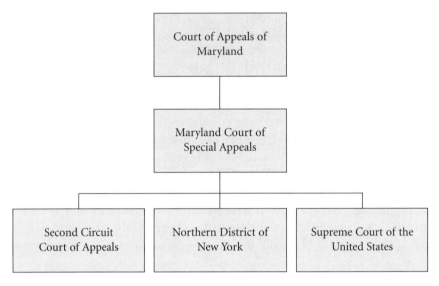

Figure 3. Maryland Hierarchy of Courts

ber also that we're only talking about questions of substantive law here. When it comes to questions of procedure—and questions of procedure can have a big influence on the outcome of a case—the federal courts rely on their own rules. So in matters of procedure, things would revert to the way they're shown in Figure 2. This might all seem complicated now, but it will become second nature to you very quickly.

This discussion so far has been about theory. In practice, even substantive issues are rarely aligned exactly like this. Almost any practicing lawyer will tell you that the federal trial court is going to pay more attention to the Supreme Court and the Second Circuit than to another federal court, and that might be accurate (although the Supreme Court will rarely have much useful to say about pure matters of state law, so its involvement in this hypothetical situation is more theoretical than realistic). Everyone will agree that federal courts are required to act as if they were state courts when they are called on to try cases under state laws. That puts a heavy burden on federal judges; not only must they decide cases based on federal law, they can be—and often are—asked to decide cases as if they were judges in any one of the various states.

The appeal of a case heard by a federal district court under state law goes to the appropriate Court of Appeals—the Second Circuit in this example—and not to the state appellate courts, because even though state law is binding, state courts have no jurisdiction over federal courts. And remember that the various procedural rules the trial court will use in hearing the case—the rules of civil procedure, for example, and the rules of evidence—will be the federal rules as well. If the case ever makes its way to the relevant Court of Appeals, that court will be required to act as though it were a state court also and will be bound by the decisions of the state's highest court.

All this can get sticky when the federal courts are asked to interpret an issue that hasn't been decided by the state court, especially in this country, where a civil war was fought over the issue of how much autonomy states have and how much authority the federal system has over the states. Mercifully, there is an escape mechanism the federal courts can invoke to allow them to get advice from the state courts when a new or undecided issue of state law comes before them. They can (but aren't required to) certify the question to the relevant state's highest court. In essence, they get to ask the state court to decide the issue for them. The state court doesn't have to answer the question, and sometimes it doesn't, usually because it disagrees with the federal court that the issue hasn't already been answered. Even then, the state court's answer can be very helpful to the federal court in formulating its decision.

What happens when a state court is asked to consider a question that has constitutional implications? As you would expect, the hierarchy of authority shifts again. Let's take a look at a chart to help explain things (Figure 4). Imagine that the Circuit Court of Missouri (the trial court in that state) has been asked to rule on the question of whether a criminal defendant was properly informed of her *Miranda* rights (familiar from countless TV shows: you have the right to remain silent, and if you give up that right, anything you say can and will be used against you in a court of law. You have the right to an attorney to be present during questioning, and if you cannot afford an attorney, one will provided for you free of charge). Even though you might think everyone in the country knows these rights by memory, issues about the appropriateness of the warnings given in particular cases come up all the time. Figure 4 shows what the hierarchy of authority looks like in this case.

Most of this is predictable—the state trial court is aligned directly below the intermediate and highest state appellate courts, as you would expect—but you might be surprised to see the highest state court aligned *below* the Supreme Court here. The federal Constitution provides a floor of protection below which a state cannot go, and the Supreme Court is the court that gets to say where that floor is located and what protections we have. No state court can overrule the Supreme Court when it comes to questions of these protections.

You might also be surprised to see that there's no place in the diagram for the relevant Court of Appeals (the Eighth Circuit in Missouri's case), and that's because although the Eighth Circuit's decisions would be binding on the federal district courts in Missouri's Eastern and Western districts, it doesn't have

Figure 4. Hierarchy of Authority in Miranda Rights Example

any direct authority over the state's courts—only the Supreme Court has that power.

C. Persuasive Authority

Up to now, this chapter has discussed binding authority—the situation where one court's decisions require lower courts to rule in the same way. You should be able to piece together on whom a particular court's decisions will be binding. Of course, you should remember that all court decisions—even those from the lowest court—are binding on the litigants appearing before it.

So all decisions are binding on someone, even if they just bind the parties in a particular case. If a decision isn't binding on someone who wasn't a party to the suit, does it have any value? The answer, like so many answers you will hear in law school, is "it depends."

The bottom line is that there is no bottom line for persuasive authority; all decisions that aren't binding on a court are "persuasive" to a degree, and there's no measure for how much, or how little, a court will be persuaded by a non-binding opinion. A federal district judge might be persuaded to follow another federal district judge's opinion if that judge is from the same district. If judge A knows judge B to be a brilliant jurist with a wealth of experience in a particular area, judge A might be inclined to follow judge B's lead in that area, or judge A might think judge B is a know-nothing airhead and would never agree with judge B, even on the time of day. One state court might be persuaded that a federal Court of Appeals decision perfectly captures the law in a particular area, and another state court would never consider following the lead of a federal court in anything.

This is where lawyers' advocacy skills come into play. A lawyer who finds an opinion that perfectly supports a client's position but isn't binding on the court in which the case is being decided, must find ways of persuading the deciding court to follow the reasoning in the opinion, even though it isn't required to do so. There are ways to do this, and you will learn them in your legal writing class, particularly when you begin the discussion of persuasive writing.

For now, here is the most important information you can take away from this section: *not all decisions are equal.* In other words, if you are an advocate, and you find a decision that supports your position, that doesn't mean that you can rely on it. You can only rely with certainty on those decisions that are mandatory or binding on the court to whom you are writing. Any other decision is persuasive, to a greater or lesser degree, and must be handled with care.

There is a mistake made by many law students and many lawyers as well. They think that because a decision supports their position, they can drop it into a brief or argument without regard to its precedential authority. Don't fall into this trap. There are few things that irritate judges more than being told that a court with no authority over them decided something one way and so they should decide the issue the same way. That doesn't mean you cannot use the case you have found, but it does mean you should be careful with it. In the meantime, try this exercise to help you with the hierarchy of authority.

> **Exercise:** For every case you read, or every opinion you read about in the press, analyze who the deciding court was, which courts this opinion will bind (what courts are aligned directly below it), and what courts will in turn bind this court if the opinion is appealed. Don't worry about the specific names of the courts, just think about levels. For example, if you read about a decision from the Seventh Circuit Court of Appeals, consider if the decision will be binding on state courts and/or federal district courts within the Seventh Circuit's geographical boundaries, and what the Supreme Court's influence on the

decision might be. For each story about court opinions you read in the press, decide whether the reporter accurately describes on whom the decision will be binding or whether there are some omissions or mistakes.

11

The Legislative Branch

Once again, you may recognize this information, which you have likely known since elementary school. If you don't know this material as well as you would like, be aware that we only glide over the surface of it here. You will talk more about the role of the legislature and its importance to legal research in your legal research and writing classes, and you cover the legislative issues more extensively in your doctrinal classes. I only be talking about the federal legislative process here; remember that there's a parallel (and equally important) legislature in every state. For now, this is a very quick tour through the legislative process and its importance to law students.

A. The Organization of the Federal Legislature

The federal legislature is known as *Congress*, and it has a bicameral structure: the lower chamber is the House of Representatives and the upper chamber is the Senate. Predictably enough, those who sit in the House are called "Representatives" and those who sit in the Senate are "Senators."

The name "Congress" actually refers to the meeting of legislatures, and these meetings are numbered so we can differentiate one from another. The 110th Congress convened in January 2007, the 111th Congress began in January 2009, and so on. There is a new Congress every two years.

The number of Representatives for each state is determined by the population of that state. There are presently 435 members of the House of Representatives, led by the Speaker of the House. Each state has two Senators, led by the President of the Senate (the Vice President of the United States) and a President Pro Tempore (usually known as the President Pro Tem). Congress meets in the U.S. Capitol building in Washington, D.C. Both the Speaker and the President Pro Tem are elected by the legislators in the House and Senate, respectively.

B. Congressional Power

Representatives and Senators are often colloquially and loosely referred to in the media as "lawmakers," and that is their principal function, although they do some other things as well. Senators approve (or not) presidential appointments, for example, and the House can impeach governmental officers, although the Senate actually conducts the impeachment trial, which is a separate process. The Constitution spells out the nature and limitations of congressional power in Article I.

C. The Legislative Process

It has been said that the two things one never wants to see made are sausages and laws. But while most people don't have a good impression of the way laws are made, lawyers should be thankful for the legislative process in this country because it generates a vast amount of information, a lot of which is very useful to us in our jobs. I cannot explain everything that happens in the legislative process or every document created during that process in this short overview. In general, you should note that each public step in the process will be memorialized, and each legislative document has the potential to be researched and used for some purpose later.

One of the difficulties in describing the legislative process lies in its flexibility. There is no required body that generates legislation; anyone can write a bill—you, me, Representatives, and Senators. And there is no set way legislation must pass through the system. A bill can be introduced in either the House or the Senate, and its passage, once introduced, is subject to an endless number of procedural stages that might (but need not) be invoked to facilitate or impede its progress. Although I can describe the passage of one hypothetical piece of legislation, you should remember that little legislation follows the same path.

Let's imagine bill H.50. What's it for? It doesn't matter—whatever you would like it to be for. We are concerned with the *process* here. Because it has an "H," you probably assume that it's been introduced in the House, and you would be correct. If it was first introduced in the Senate, it would, predictably enough, be called S. something (probably not 50, because the number of pieces of legislation in the House and Senate don't track each other).

Once introduced, legislation is usually referred to a committee, which then usually refers the bill to a subcommittee. That's where a lot of legislative work takes place—much more so than on the floor of the House or Senate. The subcommittee can do a number of things, one of which is to hold hearings on the bill. It will likely hear testimony from those in favor and those who are op-posed to the legislation, and many of those testifying also submit written doc-umentation to support their testimony. It's all public record (unless the hearings are sealed, which is unusual), and it can all be very useful to lawyers. If you dis-cover that an expert witness for the other side in a lawsuit, for example, testi-fied on a relevant issue some years ago, you can find the expert's testimony and supporting documents and probe them for potential inconsistencies with the position the expert takes in your case.

Assuming that all goes well with H.50—and this is a big assumption, as most legislation dies a quiet death in committee—the subcommittee will rec-ommend passage to the committee, which will, in turn, recommend passage to the House. Because that recommendation comes in the form of a report (more documentation), the process is sometimes colloquially referred to as "reporting" the bill out to the House.

Once H.50 has been reported out, the House can debate its merits and, as-suming the best for this legislation, vote to adopt it. At this point, the whole tortuous process begins again in the Senate. Almost inevitably, the chamber that gets the legislation second will make some changes to it—possibly some major changes and sometimes just minor ones. No matter how significant these changes might be, the legislation exists in two different versions and that can-not continue. The bill is referred to a conference committee, made up of mem-bers of both the House and Senate, to hash out the differences between the versions and to come up with a single version that is a result of compromise.

Assuming that a compromise can be reached (and assuming that anyone can recognize the original bill, now that it's been changed several times), the language of the final version goes to both the House and Senate for approval. Assuming that the legislation receives that approval, it goes on to the Presi-dent.

Of course, the process isn't over yet. The President can sign (which is what usually happens). He can decline to do anything in which case the legislation becomes law in ten days (not including Sundays—counting rules are very im-portant!) unless Congress adjourns within ten days; if that happens, the leg-islation is effectively dead (the so-called pocket veto). Third, the President can veto the legislation. If it is vetoed, the legislation goes back to the house where it originated (the House, in our example) and if first the House and then the Senate vote, by two-thirds majority, to override the veto, the legislation be-comes law without the President's signature.

That's a very abbreviated tour of the legislative process and it's not absolutely crucial that you know this before you come to law school. This is all basic civics, and your professors might assume that you have at least this baseline of information, so if you have any insecurity about of this material, you might want to review it a couple of times and maybe look for a source that describes the process in a little more detail before you come to law school. Unlike sausages, the more you know about the legislative process, the better you'll be able to digest your class discussion.

> **Exercise:** Find newspaper or news magazine stories about legislation and see if you can predict what process that legislation has followed to reach its present position. What will happen next? Whom do you think drafted the legislation? What role, if any, do you think the Supreme Court might play in the future of this legislation?

12

The Executive Branch

The most prominent member of the Executive Branch of the federal government is, of course, the President of the United States. But prominence isn't everything, and some other members of the Executive Branch are possibly more important to you, even though you might not realize it. These are the people who work for the various regulatory agencies that perform the day-to-day work of the Executive Branch departments and agencies—the Food and Drug Administration (Department of Health and Human Services), Federal Student Aid (Department of Education), and the Occupational Safety and Health Administration (Department of Labor), for example. These agencies—and independent government agencies—do work and promulgate regulations that likely have at least as significant an impact on your daily lives as lawyers and as citizens than do the actions of the President.

A. Organization

The powers of the Executive Branch of the federal government are set out in Article II of the Constitution. Of course, each state has its own Executive Branch as well, with powers defined by the state's constitution. Article II assigns to the President the responsibility to make sure that the laws are faithfully executed; the executive departments and the agencies created under them are the mechanisms by which this constitutional mandate is carried out. The head of each department sits on the Cabinet.

The President has other responsibilities in addition to the management of the departments and agencies. Among other things, the President has the power to sign legislation into law (or not sign it, or veto), make treaties, and pardon criminals who have been convicted of crimes against the federal government. Under the checks and balances approach embodied in the Constitution, most of the President's actions are subject to review by Congress.

B. The Regulatory Process

Regulations are the nuts and bolts of federal regulatory practices, and the promulgation, interpretation, and enforcement of federal regulations takes up the bulk of the energies of the extended Executive Branch. Those regulations can affect you in ways you might not have considered; if you have ever been to a doctor's office, for example, and had your tongue held down by a tongue depressor while the doctor looked at your throat, you have come into contact with a medical device as defined and specified by federal regulations promulgated by the Food and Drug Administration (FDA).

The range and scope of federal regulations is breathtaking, and you will learn more about the process by which they come into existence during the research phase of your legal research and writing classes. Here is a simplified version of the process, just to orient you in the administrative world.

Although agencies are part of the Executive Branch, they can't actually do anything without having some power granted to them by the legislature, which comes in the form of enabling legislation. That legislation says, in essence, that there is a need for an agency to enforce or implement the provisions of some legislation, and the power to do this resides in a particular agency. This legislation gives the agency the authority to do its work but also limits the scope of what the agency can and cannot do.

As with legislation, the kernel of a regulation can come from anywhere. Regulations are proposed by the agency granted the power to work in a particular area—with medical devices, for example, the relevant agency is the FDA. But agency jurisdiction is a result of function, not form. For example, if a particular medical device posed a hazard when transported by air, the Federal Aviation Administration (under the Department of Transportation) would be the agency to promulgate regulations that defined how and if that device could be carried on a plane.

The easiest way to think of the relationship between legislation and regulation is to think of the relationship between high-level political decisions and their implementation. In World War II, for example, politicians decided that the United States should declare war on Germany, but the series of orders that moved individual soldiers and pieces of material around to enable U.S. involvement in the D-Day invasion of France in 1944 issued not from Congress or the White House but from a fairly lowly army office. Similarly, Congress and the President might agree on the importance of some legislation and the broad political aims embodied by it, but they typically leave the details of enforcing that legislation to an administrative agency.

An agency meets its responsibilities by promulgating regulations, or rules, that are designed to meet the goals of specific pieces of legislation. In practical terms, they have the same mandatory effect on behavior as laws enacted by Congress or court decisions—you can no more decide to not obey a federal regulation than you can decide to ignore a court ruling or not follow the requirements of legislation.

The process of generating those regulations is a little different from that of court decisions or lawmaking. The agency usually must propose the new regulations, publish them, and invite comments. These comments are often copious, and although they usually come from businesses or industries that will be affected by the new regulation, they can come from private citizens as well. The agency then considers the comments and might amend the proposed regulations, if the comments reveal consequences the agency hadn't anticipated, for example. The agency might offer these revisions for further comment, or it might publish the regulations as final, but it does so before the regulations actually take effect to give everyone who might be affected time to conform their behavior to the regulations before they find themselves in violation.

As you might imagine, this generates a substantial amount of information, and all of it is published. Proposed new regulations and changes to established regulations happen every day and are published almost every day in the *Federal Register*, which also publishes final regulations. Once they are final, regulations are codified and published in the Code of Federal Regulations (CFR).

The CFR is a truly massive work and is the principal piece of evidence for those who argue that this country is overregulated. It is also a symbol of a tremendous amount of work by a large body of people and a tangible sign that we live in complicated times and in a complex society. Whether you think of the United States as over or underregulated, it's important to remember that those are philosophical and political concerns. As citizens, you have no choice but to obey the regulations in the CFR; as lawyers, your job is to find, interpret, propose revisions to, and occasionally challenge the validity of those regulations. Like them or hate them, they are a crucial part of our personal and professional lives.

> **Exercise:** Think of all the federal regulations that might have affected your life today. What agencies might have promulgated those regulations? Select one of these agencies and look for its Web site. Can you find any information on the regulation you think might have affected you?

13

What Else Is There to Do?

Let's assume you have read this book—actively—up until this chapter, you have done all the exercises, you are briefing at least one case a day, and there is still another month to go before law school starts. Alternatively, let's assume that you've glanced through the book and have decided, for whatever reason, that you're not going to spend much time reading it or doing the exercises. Or perhaps you're halfway through the book and you need a break.

For anyone who falls into any of these groups, there's an important question to ask: is there anything else to do? Yes. *Lots.* Here is a short and nonexclusive list of ten things prospective law students could do to help them get ready for law school, even if they didn't do any of the things described previously. Try any one of these things, try a few, or try them all. Any of them will make you a better law student, and some of them might make you a better person. They will certainly make you more employable during and after law school.

A. Read

I have made some suggestions of things you might want to read throughout this book, but if you don't want to read those things, try this: read *anything*, read *a lot*, and read *actively*. How much is a lot? Two hours a day at a minimum, three or four if you can. Though it's best to read something that is well written and intellectually stimulating, you can learn a lot about writing and improve your writing skills by reading almost anything.

The important thing is to read *actively*, not passively. If you let words pass by your eyes, you are not doing anything except taking up time. Although that might not seem like the worst thing to do in the summer before law school, it's a lost opportunity. If you asked almost any first-year law student facing exams if they wish they had better studying and reading skills, without taking any time away from their revision schedule, they probably would tell you that they would leap at the chance.

That's what you have the opportunity to do, before you go to school. You can do it lying on a beach, sitting in a comfortable chair, almost anywhere. But you have to concentrate: you can't have any distractions or interruptions while you are reading—no email, no texting, no music. You have to be active in your reading. Ask questions of the text and the writer, and assess how well the writer does in answering those questions. If you were the writer of what you're reading, how would you have written it differently to make it better? Would you have chosen the same word(s) to encapsulate that thought? Why did the writer chose the words he or she did and not the ones you would have chosen? What will the writer say next? If you were wrong in your prediction, why? Try to summarize what you have read during the day to someone else. Can you recall specific details, or are you missing some important elements? Is your retelling structured in the same way as what you have been reading, or did you choose a different narrative structure? Did your approach work? Let your responses to these questions today tell you how you're going to read tomorrow.

B. Read American History

If you're looking for something specific but nonlegal to read this summer, try a general history of the United States. There's probably no better nonspecialist way to prepare yourself for law school than understanding something about the way this country was founded and how it developed.

Some might say, in fact, that there's no clear distinction between American history and American law. These people see the law as a natural outgrowth of this country's culture and beliefs, shaped by its history. To them, U.S. laws tell a powerful story of history, just as history is a reflection of a country's laws. Whatever the merits of this opinion, it's impossible to see the law and American history as anything but inextricably linked together. The country's founding, the Civil War and its aftermath, the development of the market economy, the upheavals of the Great Depression, and the great social debates of today all have legal implications. The better you understand the history of this country, the better you'll understand its laws.

I'm not saying you need a degree in American history to do well in law school (although having one certainly wouldn't hurt). I am saying that a basic understanding of what has happened in this country, when, and why it happened will help you in law school and will help you become a better rounded, more interesting person. That's the sort of person law firms hire.

C. Compare the Way Stories Are Reported

If you don't want to learn about American history, at least learn something about current events. There is always something interesting going on in this country: either the economy is going up or it's going down; there's almost always a judicial opening in the federal judiciary—sometimes a Supreme Court position is vacant, but there are usually multiple openings on the circuit Courts of Appeals and in the various district courts; the President and Congress are always up to something; and so on.

Don't just inform yourself about what's going on in the country—try to go deeper. Pick a current story that looks as if it will be around for a while and compare the way the different news outlets talk about it: read multiple newspaper versions of the story (many newspapers are available on the Internet, as well as in your local library), read news magazine coverage of the story, watch several TV stations' coverage of the story, listen to what radio news—and radio talk shows—have to say about it. In short, try to read, listen to, and watch as much as you can about the story.

Once you are engrossed in the details, start to listen to the tone of the reporting and the commentary. Some news outlets and commentators are very clear about their political bias. Some either don't want you to think they are biased or at least try to disguise their biases. Can you identify their biases anyway? Don't ask whether you agree with the slant these outlets are putting on the news: it's important to have views, of course, but that's not the purpose of this exercise. Rather, the goal here is to hone your sensitivity to language, tone and voice, and rhetoric. What techniques do the reporters and commentators use to persuade you either of one view or another or that they don't have a bias? (Remember that it takes just as much rhetorical skill—perhaps even more—to persuade you that a writer is neutral as it does to persuade you of one position or another.) Once you can identify the techniques the writers or commentators use, judge how effective they are. Are they using techniques you can use in your legal writing or in oral argument? Again, it doesn't matter whether you agree or disagree with the positions these people are taking; we are just examining technique here. There's almost always something to be learned if you pay attention.

D. Read a Newspaper Front to Back Every Day

If you don't want to do the work to compare stories reported by numerous outlets, try to read the work of at least one outlet every day by reading a newspaper front to back. That means reading about the things that interest you and the things that don't particularly grab your attention.

For example, if you are a sports fan but couldn't care less about theater or dance, by all means read the baseball and basketball coverage voraciously, but read the theater and dance reviews as well. Don't passively read the stories you're not interested in, read them actively. If the writer uses words or concepts with which you are unfamiliar, research them until you understand everything the writer talked about.

The purpose of this exercise isn't to educate you about subjects you don't find interesting (although there's a fair argument to be made that a rounded, intelligent person should be interested in everything the typical newspaper reports about) but to get you into the habit of learning things you are unfamiliar with. Law probably isn't like anything else you have studied, and you will probably find parts of it fascinating and parts of it—to be polite—less so. You will have to learn it all, though, so it's better to get into the habit of learning things that are uninteresting and unfamiliar to you sooner rather than later.

Even if you find the law entirely fascinating, it's almost certain that when you get out into practice, there will be aspects of your clients' cases that you find less than enthralling. You cannot tell clients, though, that you think what they do is boring so you didn't learn enough about it to make a convincing argument to a court, or didn't pay attention to the drafting of a contract because the sale of this particular widget isn't interesting to you.

The skill of learning something with which you're unfamiliar—or something you find uninteresting—quickly and well is a skill that will stand you in good stead in law school and law practice. In any case, you might find that a director's concept for an Ibsen play or the theory of the infield fly rule is more interesting than you thought at first. Stranger things have happened.

E. Watch C-SPAN for an Hour Each Day

It might not seem like the most exciting thing to do, but this country offers its citizens an almost unprecedented chance to watch government in action, and that's something we should all do from time to time. The availability of the C-SPAN cable channel means that we don't have to travel to Washington, D.C., to avail ourselves of this opportunity; we can sit in the comfort of our own homes and watch politicians do what they do.

For lawyers in training, there are several reasons to watch C-SPAN on a regular basis. First, and most obviously, you get a front-row seat to the system of government you will soon be swearing to uphold and will be studying in depth.

This is literally the Constitution in action, and the more you understand the practical application of the theory you'll study in law school, the more sense everything will make to you. Second, there isn't a better way to inform yourself about the important political issues of the day than seeing what politicians say about those issues. Better still, of course, is to combine your watching with good reporting about what happened in Congress so you can compare your reactions with those of the reporters and see whether you agree with the published reports.

Third, and perhaps most important, you will have a chance to watch and critique the performances of men and woman whose job it is to persuade you of a position by the quality of their oral performance. That sounds a lot like what you will be doing as a lawyer. There are differences, of course—politicians often make speeches, and that's something lawyers don't tend to do (despite what many people think, opening statements and closing arguments *aren't* speeches). All lawyers (not just litigators) have to make oral presentations from time to time, and you can learn a lot about good and bad presentation style by watching politicians at work. You should watch their posture, their use of notes, the fluency of their presentation, the way they use (or don't use) visual aids like charts, and listen to their rhetoric as they try to persuade you of a position. As always, don't worry about whether you agree with them—that's a personal question and you're learning about professional skills when you do this. Consider how they are going about the process of trying to persuade you, and if you see a technique you like—or dislike—make a note of it to see if you can adapt or avoid it when you start to make oral presentations yourself.

F. Go to Court and Observe

An even more direct way to learn about the presentation styles some lawyers use is to see them in action, and you can do this by going to court and watching the action. Going to court is free and can be educational and entertaining. There are some things you should know before you go.

First, remember that what you see in court is representative only of litigation, and that's something fewer lawyers are actively engaged in these days. Although most lawyers still call themselves "litigators," not many of them actually spend time in court. Litigation has become almost all to do with the pretrial work done in warehouses full of documents, conference rooms where depositions are held, and offices where pleadings and motions are written. Although litigation might still be the most popular area of legal practice, many lawyers have no professional interest in seeing the inside of a courtroom.

Even if you aren't likely to be a courtroom lawyer yourself, you will still benefit from seeing lawyers in action in the courtroom. For one thing, you'll learn how accurate—or inaccurate—TV shows portraying litigation really are. You will also learn that a lot of litigation happens without lawyers at all; many people either can't afford a lawyer or, for one reason or another, want to represent themselves. The fact that the law can (and often does) exist without our input is an important and salutary lesson about our role in society.

Second, you should know that it's quite likely you won't see much, if anything. At any large courthouse in the country, you will probably see a lot of lawyers in action during the first couple of days of the week, but you might not see anything on Fridays. Cases usually are scheduled to start on Mondays, but they can often be concluded or settled before the end of the week. Courts sometimes reserve Fridays for motions hearings, but between the time a motion is scheduled and the time it is scheduled to be heard, the lawyers might have met and resolved the issues that prompted the motion. You might have to go back a few times to see some extended lawyering.

You should also expect to be asked who you are, often by the presiding judge in the courtroom. They usually ask because one or other of the parties to litigation has invoked a rule that prevents potential witnesses from hearing the testimony of other witnesses, and often they are interested to know who's sitting in their courtroom. If you tell the judge that you're going to be a law student, you might find yourself invited to come up to the bench to have a talk about your plans; judges and lawyers are often happy to speak with someone who takes the initiative to come watch them at work.

This suggests that you should probably dress up a little before going to court. I don't mean that you should wear a business suit, but it might be better to avoid jeans and a T-shirt if you can; if there's the chance you will be speaking to a judge and some lawyers dressed in full battle gear, you will feel less self-conscious if you've taken some steps to dress appropriately.

Always remember that courthouses are filled with people who are unhappy about being there, either because they are civil litigants or criminal defendants, or because they are witnesses in trials or family members of those involved in litigation. As lawyers, we tend to look forward to trial so much that we forget that almost everyone else involved in the process is miserable that things have reached the courtroom; criminal defendants could lose and go to jail or, at best, leave with a criminal record against their name, while one side or the other in civil litigation is probably going to lose money. Almost everyone is unhappy about paying their lawyer a lot of money.

All this unhappiness means that you should be careful how you behave and speak to people you meet in the courthouse. Making jokes about how weak one side's case is to a litigant's family members isn't likely to endear you to them, and the person you ride with in the elevator might be a court watcher like yourself or the defendant in a criminal case. It's always best to keep your conversation to a minimum and watch more than you speak. If you do that, and if you keep coming back if you don't see something interesting on your first visit, you will almost certainly have a valuable and educational experience.

G. Learn Something About Culture and Social Behavior

Even if you acquire the knowledge from a newspaper, you should consider learning something about aspects of culture and social behavior with which you are unfamiliar.

In a previous section, I said that you might find aspects of theater or sport more interesting than you first expected, but you should learn about them even if you don't think you'll ever become a fan of theater or sports (or classical music, or fashion, or politics). Put simply, you're going to be mixing with people—attorneys who are senior to you and clients—who find these things important. You should know enough about a wide range of subjects to at least be able to support your end of a conversation or, at least, not embarrass yourself by behaving inappropriately in an unfamiliar setting. You don't need to know why everyone applauds at certain times at a classical music concert or at a baseball game when nothing seems to have happened; all you need to do is to wait and see how everyone else behaves and then behave the same way.

Of course, the more you do know, the better, and that's particularly true of social behavior. Lawyers find themselves at fancier restaurants and different types of parties than the ones they were used to as undergraduates. Trust me when I say that it's better to learn how to behave ahead of time in those situations. Read a book about etiquette and go to a fancy restaurant where you can practice your newly learned social skills. You will learn something useful and get a good meal into the bargain.

H. Get a Job in a Law Firm or Government Office

One of the best ways to see what life is like as a lawyer is to watch lawyers working. Although it's not likely that you'll find a law firm willing to give you legal work to do when you haven't started law school yet, you might find offices willing to give you work as a paralegal or, more likely, in the copy room or mail office.

All lawyers should remember that they are part of a chain of people who are necessary to get a client's work done. They're an important part of the chain, to be sure, but no matter how brilliant a lawyer's work product might be, it won't get written without the assistance of the more junior lawyers who did some initial research and updated the research to make sure the cited cases are still good law. It won't be reduced to writing without the secretary who types out the dictated brief, and it won't be read without the copy room staff, who print and copy it and the paralegal who ensures that it's delivered to the court and the other parties in the case. Most lawyers don't forget the important work the other people in a law office do, and the best way to make sure you're not in the minority who think that only they are important is to have been one of the nonlawyers in an office for a while.

Another, very practical reason for working in any capacity in a law office is the knowledge you will acquire about how the office machines work. This might seem like a foolish thing to say; when you're a lawyer, you might need to know how to use the computers in your office, and possibly the copy machine every now and then, but will you really need to know how the Federal Express, UPS, or mail labeling systems work? Most of the time, you won't. But now and then, you'll find yourself working at 11 p.m., with no one else in the office, and you're going to need to know how to get a document out before the start of the next business day. At a time like that, knowing how to label a package—and knowing where the last pickup of the day will be—can be invaluable knowledge. The best lawyers know when it's time to stay closeted in their offices to get their work done, and when it's time to pitch in and help with the copying, the mailing, or setting up the conference rooms for meetings and depositions. Working in a nonlegal capacity in a law office can help you learn how to do those critical jobs as well as your own.

A less tangible benefit of finding a job like this is the message it sends to prospective employers once you start looking for paying legal jobs after your first year of law school. Often, lawyers interviewing students for summer associate positions are faced with résumés that look very much the same; many students go straight from high school to an undergraduate institution and from there straight to law school, and their résumés all look alike. These students are usually highly intelligent and are able to do the legal work asked of them without difficulty, but it's difficult for a prospective employer to make any principled choices between these applicants.

An easy way to help your résumé stand out is to show prospective employers that you have had some experience working in an office. When they ask you about that experience in your interview—and they will—they will be impressed to learn that you took the initiative to find that work because you wanted to understand what life in a law office was like. Practicing lawyers know that not all aspects of legal practice are enjoyable, and they look for prospective employees who understand that as well; those younger lawyers will have much less difficulty settling into an office routine than will those who are shocked to learn of the sometimes-long hours lawyers work and the stresses that can make some days tense and difficult. Any job has these stresses from time to time, of course—there's nothing unusual about a law practice in that regard. But someone who has never experienced them before is at a significant disadvantage compared to someone who has faced them and can accept them as part of the usual life in the workplace.

I. If You Can't Get a Paying Job, Volunteer

Of course, it's best to get paid while you acquire valuable knowledge like how to use a fax machine and how to deal with workplace stress, but it can be difficult to get paying jobs in law firms, especially if you are only going to be there for a few months before going to law school. You can get the same experience, and perhaps make an even better impression on your résumé, by volunteering at a law office. Lawyers all recognize the importance of pro bono work and by showing you have a commitment to serving your community, you send a clear message that you understand this part of a lawyer's life as well.

It's best, of course, if you can find an office that can't afford your services at which to volunteer; you will get much of the same work experience if you volunteer at a large corporate law firm, but the pro bono aspect of working at a firm like that might be more difficult to demonstrate than if you worked at an inner-city clinic providing free legal services to those who can't afford to hire a lawyer. You might even find that the life led by lawyers who work at such clinics is more enjoyable, and more challenging, than the life of an associate at a corporate law firm.

J. Write

If you do nothing else in your time before coming to law school, try to make a commitment to yourself to write at least a page of text every day, on top of whatever other writing you might normally do. If you write a case brief a day or some other writing related to coming to law school, that should count. If you are not doing this, find some way to practice putting words next to each other to form sentences and convey meaning.

It's possible to get by without spending much time writing in everyday life. The writing we tend to do—sending emails and text messages for many people—is usually structured to be in short segments, often in fragments rather than full sentences. That's fine for the immediate purpose, but it doesn't help prepare you for the extensive formal writing you will have to do in law school and as lawyers. In fact, law school can often be a shock for students whose undergraduate (and sometimes even graduate) degrees didn't require much writing.

Lawyers can be defined in many ways, and perhaps the most accurate description of a lawyer is as a professional writer. In a typical year, a lawyer will write the equivalent of at least a short novel, all of it at a very high standard of technical precision and accuracy, and hardly any of it with the luxury of a professional editor. In short, lawyers write *a lot*, and the sooner you get used to the experience of writing every day, the easier the transition to the life of a professional writer will be.

Unlike the work you do as a law student and as a lawyer, you probably won't be writing for anyone in particular during your time before law school, although if you have a parent or significant other who would be willing to read something you write every day, you should leap at the chance to write for them! Even if you don't have a specific audience in mind while you write, imagine that you are writing to someone you know; it's easier to write with a specific audience in mind than to write for an undefined reader.

What should you write? It doesn't really matter—the experience of expressing yourself in written, formal English is what's important. A daily journal entry is the obvious suggestion, but try to combine that with some of the other things you're doing to get ready for law school if you can. You could, for example, write about your impressions in going to court or about things that happened to you in your job. Perhaps you could write about what you saw on C-SPAN, and the presentation techniques employed by the politicians you thought were effective or ineffective. Maybe you could write about the underlying biases you detected in the way a news story is being reported and whether you think the techniques various reporters are writing about the story could be incorporated into your legal writing style.

There are a limitless number of things you could write about, so the important thing is not to worry about *what* to write, it's to get writing. Even though no one might read it, do your best to make your work as technically perfect as possible; spell-check it, edit it for clarity and conciseness, proofread it for grammatical and punctuation errors—really try to make each finished piece of writing as perfect as possible. The habits you instill now, when there's no pressure on you, will be tremendously helpful when you're stressed out from all the work you have to accomplish. Remember that you're not writing for fun, but to improve your skills to make you a better law student and a better lawyer.

14

Conclusion

No matter how much you do to prepare yourself for law school, you will probably experience a feeling of dread on your first day. Almost every law student has a similar story to tell: you'll get the syllabi for your courses well in advance of the first class, buy your books, and sit down and spend hours reading and briefing the cases, taking notes, and generally thinking about what's coming. You'll feel pretty good about what you know.

Then comes the first day of classes. You walk into class, unpack your books and note-taking materials, maybe introduce yourself to your neighbors, look around to see if anyone looks smarter than you, and then your professor will walk in. There might be a brief introduction to the course, maybe a quick check of everyone's name and seat, and then the words everyone fears: "Ms. (or Mr.) X, would you give us the facts of …"

If your name is called, you will hear your brain say, "It's been good knowing you," and you will feel it disconnect itself from your body as it prepares to run screaming from the building. If your name is not called, you offer up silent prayers to the law school gods and sit back to listen to someone else have a public nervous attack. In neither case, though, would you likely be able to spell the name of the plaintiff in the case, never mind recite the facts and the holding.

Somehow, the facts are recited and the class starts to relax. Then the professor starts posing hypothetical questions, changing the facts a little, and asking whether the same result would occur if the facts were this way. Or that way. Or this third way. More panic. Your body temperature rises, and your breakfast seems less secure than it was ten minutes ago. As soon as you start to get used to this new style of teaching, and start to feel able to answer some of the professors' hypotheticals, the class is over, and you realize the professor offered no answers to any of the questions.

Don't worry. This happens to everyone. The only consolation is that everyone feels the same way, no matter how relaxed and calm they look on the outside. The feeling will continue, because you will hardly ever get a straight answer in class; there will be new hypotheticals and new questions each class, but no answers.

That's the way law school is. The purpose isn't to make you feel as if you don't know anything, but that usually is one of the side effects. If it helps, think of a lawyer you know or have seen on television in a commercial—the dumber the better. That person not only survived the first day of law school, he or she graduated and passed the bar as well—certainly if he or she is in practice. If that lawyer can get through law school, so can you!

The thing that often gets lost in that first day of law school, and often for many days afterward, is how smart and accomplished you are. You must be; unintelligent, incapable people simply don't get in to law schools these days. Just by virtue of the fact that you have been admitted to law school, you have already demonstrated that you're more than smart and capable enough to thrive there.

Not everyone thrives, of course. Some people flunk out, and some who graduate perform poorly. That's not because they weren't smart or weren't capable of doing well; more than likely, it's because they didn't work hard. It's not a popular message these days, but success in law school requires a lot of time-consuming hard work, and there's no substitute for taking the time to prepare intelligently for every class.

If you need a mental image to help clarify this concept, consider your favorite sports figure, musician, dancer, or performer in any medium. When you watch that person perform, what you see looks as if it's being done with consummate ease, flawless execution, and often a calm, relaxed demeanor. What you're not seeing are the years of practice, repetitive, boring, and unglamorous exercise—often being botched time and again—before that level of skill was reached. No matter how naturally talented someone is, a degree of commitment to the task is essential for one to marvel at the finished product. In fact, it's often the most talented performer—the one you would imagine would need the practice the least—who puts in the most time getting ready to perform.

What's true in sports and the arts is also true in law. No law student, no matter how intelligent and no matter how capable, was ever able to recite the facts of a case or defend a position against a professor's barrage of hypotheticals without a great deal of thoughtful preparation. It might look easy in class, but it's the product of a lot of work.

This book was designed to help you understand the nature of that work and help you prepare to start doing it once you get to law school. If you follow through on at least some of its suggestions, and if you keep working once school starts and keep up your good work habits after the pressure of school starts to build, you will be fine. The good news, but also the bad news, is that it's all up to you.

That's all in the future. For now, enjoy your time before law school starts, and try to prepare yourself in an efficient, methodical manner for the challenge ahead. Always remember: lawyers are privileged members of society who wield a tremendous amount of power on behalf of their clients. Very soon, you will have an incredible opportunity to influence society and work on behalf of people who rely on your skill and counsel. Congratulations on your acceptance of a lawyer's responsibility, and welcome to law school!

Index